Precision Horse Training with Positive Reinforcement

12 Thin-Sliced Groundwork Plans

by

Hertha James

Powerword Publications

Muddy Horse Coaching

hertha.james@xtra.co.nz

www.herthamuddyhorse.com

Copyright © 2018 Hertha James

Disclaimer of Liability

Being with horses can be a hazardous activity. It is possible for participants and/or their horses to sustain injury. Hertha James and her associates will not assume any liability for your activities with a horse. This book provides information that may not be suitable for every person or every horse. No warranty is given regarding the suitability of this information to you or any other individual acting under your guidance.

Risk Radar: it's important, around horses, to have your risk radar on at all times.

James, Hertha. *Precision Horse Training with Positive Reinforcement: 12 Thin-Sliced Groundwork Plans*

Cover photo: Boots during a gymnastic exercise session.

Some illustrations are taken from video footage, so sharpness was sacrificed to capture specific moments.

Dedication

This book is dedicated to all the people on Facebook clicker training groups who take the time to share their highs and lows. Their stories give both new and experienced clicker trainers across the world access to many viewpoints. And they help alleviate the isolation that often accompanies 'being different' from the mainstream.

Acknowledgements

Thank you to my intrepid copy editors and sounding boards in Canada, Bonnie Boon and Colleen Spence.

This was the year of my double knee replacement. As well as the care from family, my horse, Boots, helped enormously to make me persevere through the pain of recovering the bend in my knees and strengthening the traumatized leg muscles.

When she realized that I could only walk extremely slowly, she adjusted her pace to mine when we moved together in the arena.

When I used her arena obstacles to do my exercises, she often stood with me. Now, many months later, my knees are good enough for us to resume our early morning walks together.

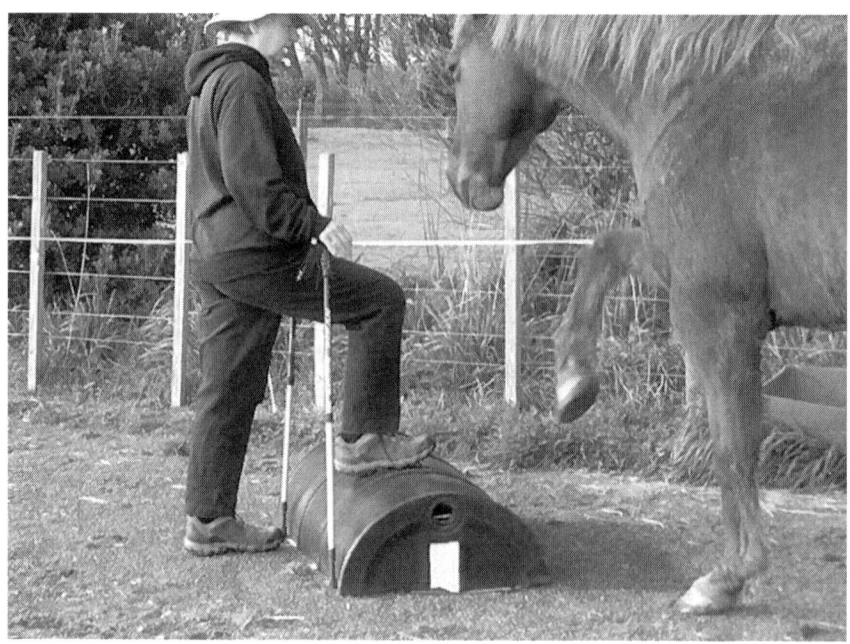

Boots helping me with my physiotherapy.

Table of Contents

Dedication   3

   About the Author   9

   Other Books   10

   Free YouTube Video Clip Links   11

   Glossary Note   12

Chapter One

   If You are New to Clicker Training Horses   13

      Background   13

      How Does the Horse Know When He is Right?   15

      Horse-Human Disfunction   16

      Resetting Tasks   17

   The Key Stages of New Learning   18

      Acquisition   18

      Fluency   19

      Generalization   20

      Maintenance   22

   Basics of Effective Clicker Training   23

      Materials: Gear Checklist   24

      Method   29

Practice with a Person   31

With the Horse   33

A. Touching a Target to Earn a Click&treat   33

B. Lunging for the Treat   36

C. Developing Good Table Manners   40

D. Targeting: next sessions   42

E. Capturing and Free-Shaping Behaviors   45

F. Guided Shaping   48

G. Counter Conditioning   49

Thin-Slicing for Individual Education Programs   51

Successive Approximations   53

Signals   54

Pauses, Dwell Time and Down Time   56

Parameters   57

Summary   59

Chapter Two

Parking with Duration   61

Chapter Three

'Zero Intent' and 'Intent'   69

Chapter Four

    Seeking the Horse's 'Consent' Signals   77

        What are 'Okay' Signals?   79

        'Okay to Repeat' Using Nose Targets   82

        'Okay to Proceed' with Mat Foot Targets   89

        Horse Specific 'Okay' Body Language Signals   93

Chapter Five

    Targeting Body Parts to the Hand   99

Chapter Six

    20 Steps Exercise   109

Chapter Seven

    Soft Response to Rope Signals   119

Chapter Eight

    The Finesse Back-Up   133

Chapter Nine

    Backing Up Shoulder-to-Shoulder   149

Chapter Ten

    Willing Whoa with a Voice Signal   159

Chapter Eleven

    Precision with a Rail   169

Chapter Twelve

    Changing Sides in Motion   179

Chapter Thirteen

    Precision Leading Using 'Gates'   187

Conclusion   199

Appendix   192

    HorseGym with Boots Series   **202**

    Thin-Slicing Examples   **207**

    Free-Shaping Examples   **208**

Reference List   210

Glossary   212

About the Author

Hertha James grew up in Calgary east of the Rocky Mountains in Alberta, Canada. Her lifelong passion for horses began at age six riding a big black horse. Animals of all kinds have always been an important part of her work and leisure.

Hertha's career with animals began with a zoology degree and includes working as a zookeeper in Calgary and Wellington, New Zealand, as well as handling wild and exotic species for a movie production company.

Her animal experiences stood her in good stead when she changed careers to become a high school teacher of science and biology. Her classrooms always contained a menagerie ranging from axolotls to quail.

Hertha's other passion, the creation of teaching and learning resources, grew from her experiences as a teacher.

Teaching science to teenagers for 23 years honed her ability to structure information clearly. It taught her how to build new knowledge in small steps and integrate it with the information and beliefs already held by her students.

Hertha applies the same successful strategy to teaching horses and their handlers. She shows that horse training goals can be reached when valid starting points are based on gentle experimentation followed by good planning to reach realistic goals.

Other Books

The following books are also available from Amazon as hard copy or e-books. They contain much background material and specific Training Plans. You can find them any time by putting the author's name (Hertha James) into the Amazon search engine.

- *How to Begin Equine Clicker Training: Improve Horse-Human Communication*

- *Conversations with Horses: An In-depth look at the Signals & Cues between Horses and their Handlers*

- *Walking with Horses: The Eight Leading Positions*

- *Learn Universal Horse Language: No Ropes*

- *How to Create Good Horse Training Plans: The Art of Thin-Slicing*

- *Confident Horse Foot Care Using Reward Reinforcement*

- *Load Your Horse Confidently Using Reward Reinforcement*

- *Teach Your Horse Long-Reining with Reward Reinforcement*

If you prefer e-books but don't have a Kindle reader, Amazon has a free Kindle reader which can be downloaded to any computer, tablet or smartphone.

Free YouTube Video Clip Links

You can find my YouTube channel with a search for *Hertha MuddyHorse*. Please see the Appendix for a comprehensive list of titles. Relevant video clips are mentioned throughout the book. The clips are kept short for easy viewing and quick revision. There are a number of playlists with a wide variety of topics.

These playlists mainly relate to the ideas in this book:

1. *Obstacle Challenges for Clicker Trainers*: the items in this playlist are dated with the month they were produced. They were first published on my Facebook page of the same name, but things rapidly get 'lost' there. Many of the clips for the book are in this playlist.

2. *HorseGym with Boots*: these are numbered. For example, if you would like to view Clip #132, simply put "*#132 HorseGym with Boots*" into the YouTube search engine and it should take you there. Each title starts with hashtag followed by its number.

3. *Starting Clicker Training:* contains clips about first starting out with clicker training.

4. *Free-Shaping*: These clips only have names. To find one, click on the playlist and scroll down to find the title that you want.

5. *Thin-Slicing*: These clips also only have names so please scroll down the list to find the title you want to view.

Glossary Note:

The glossary is at the very back of the book, to make finding it easy.

Items in the text marked with an asterisk (*) are described in the glossary.

For ease of reading, I refer to horses generally as 'he' unless I am writing about a specific mare or filly.

Keeping or re-gaining the horse's confidence is always more important that accomplishing a task right now.

Chapter One

If You are New to Clicker Training Horses

If you are an experienced clicker trainer, you may want to move on to Chapter Two. However, it can be a good exercise to occasionally review the basics.

Parts of this chapter are included in some of my other books because the foundations of safety and good treat delivery underpin every new task we want to teach with clicker training.

Background

Being grazers and browsers with small stomachs, horses are always on the lookout for a tasty morsel, so it is easy for them to fall in love with clicker training.

My theory is that horses consider working for food rewards as one more way to extract nourishment from their environment. They already graze, browse, pull hay from slow-feeding nets or bins, roll treat balls around, dig through snow for grass and in times of starvation, dig up roots. So, from a horse's point of view, learning other specific behaviors that will result in food is a continuation of their existing food-seeking continuum.

Working for a food reward (even a tiny one like a strip of carrot) activates one of the most powerful seeking systems in the deepest part of the mammal brain.

Of course, horses also learn by seeking out what will *release pressure**, i.e. the discomfort-comfort dynamic. But the motivating factor of a *food reward* allows us to add a whole new dimension to our training. The horse can become proactive in his communication with us. It's also much more fun to work with.

By taking time to thin-slice the skills Boots needed to confidently move through a solid hanging curtain, she was able to relax with this task.

Once you get into the habit of having treats with you, and your horse becomes clicker-savvy, you can use the mark and reward* clicker training system to teach your horse new things or to refine tasks that the horse already knows.

Playing with gymnastic ground games gives us a platform to expand existing skills and develop new ones while keeping our horse alert and moving.

Clicker training means that we are looking for moments to reward, rather than moments to correct.

Boots is receiving her treat after a click for a nice halt following a 'whoa' voice signal upon reaching the mat.

Once they are clicker-savvy*, horses show a strong desire to work for a food reward. They love the click&treat dynamic because the click (or special word/sound) is timed to tell them exactly what they did that will earn another treat. Horses love clarity. They like to be right in the same way as we like to be right.

The mark and reward (clicker training) system removes much of the guess-work horses face when we use only the discomfort-comfort or 'release reinforcement*' system.

How Does the Horse Know When He is Right?

When we use clicker training, the horse has three ways of knowing he is doing what we would like him to do.

1. The horse hears the click which tells him that he's just done something that earns a treat. He can go into treat retrieval mode.

2. The treat is a pleasant consequence that rewards his attention and effort. The horse is motivated to repeat

the action to receive another click&treat. The treat gives the horse a reason to interact with the handler. He understands that there is something positive in it for him.

3. Once the horse knows the gesture, touch, voice or body language signal related to a task, he knows he is 'right' when the signal stops. Signal pressure can be very light once the horse understands what we want, but its removal is still highly significant.

Horse-Human Disfunction

Most horse-human dysfunction is due to lack of clarity from the human side of the relationship due to one or more of the following reasons.

1. Our behavior around the horse is inconsistent.
2. Our signals to ask the horse to do something are inconsistent, poorly thought out or poorly taught.
3. We are not able to read the horse's body language well enough to understand what he is communicating to us about his physical, emotional or mental state.

Most horses are happy to comply with our requests if:

- We teach what we want thoughtfully and carefully in a way that the horse can understand.
- We ensure our signals are clear and consistent.
- We have well-timed click&treat and/or release of signal pressure.
- We teach at a pace that the horse can absorb; not too fast.
- We teach at a pace that maintains the horse's interest; not too slowly.

Clicker training* means that we are looking for the moments to reward, rather than moments to correct.

As the handler gets better and better at thin-slicing* a large task into its smallest teachable parts, it becomes easier and easier for the horse to learn by being continually successful. It's this aspect of learning that makes a horse look forward to his sessions.

Resetting Tasks

Rather than correct something that did not go well, we learn to reset* a task without placing a negative value judgement on what the horse just did. This makes a huge difference to how horses perceive their training. As mentioned earlier, clicker-savvy* horses often don't want their sessions to end. The positive vibrations that go with good clicker training make it fun rather than a chore.

Clicker training gives us a way to let the horse know instantly, by the sound of the marker signal* (click), when he is right. It takes away much of the guessing horses must do as they strive to read our intent* (which is often fuzzy to them). A horse's perceptions and world view are quite different from human perception and world view.

The remainder of this chapter outlines a method for introducing yourself and your horse to clicker training.

Considerably more detail is available in my book, *How to Begin Equine Clicker Training: Improve Horse-Human Communication.*

Horses begin to look forward to their clicker training sessions and often don't want them to finish.

The Key Stages of New Learning

Acquisition, Fluidity, Generalization and Maintenance

Acquisition

Acquisition includes getting our head around how we will ask for a unique behavior and then explaining what we want to the horse.

The way we first present new material to the horse is crucial. As much as possible, we want the horse to be continuously successful.

It's helpful to practice our ideas and techniques first on a person standing in for the horse. If you are lucky enough to have an experienced horse, it also helps to work out techniques with him before moving on to a novice horse.

Even a well-educated, experienced horse appreciates learning new things in small slices. This allows him to build confidence and expertise with each step toward being able to carry out the whole task smoothly with one click&treat at the end.

We always begin with low-key experimentation to see what the horse can already offer. We may find that some of the basic elements in our Individual Education Program (IEP)* are missing or not quite good enough. We might find some major training holes that need to be addressed.

For example, before we can teach our horse to weave a series of objects, have we taught him to confidently walk with us on a loose lead rope? Does he easily stay beside us, stepping off when we step off, halting when we halt and turning when we turn?

Gentle experimentation may also lead us to discover that the horse already has a solid foundation on which we can easily build a new task.

Fluency

Once we have created an Individual Education Program* and carefully taken the horse through it, we have acquired the ability to carry out a specific behavior together.

If the task is part of daily general care and recreation, such as safety around gates, the horse will have ample opportunity to use the new behavior often and receive reinforcement for it. His response to the signal will become more fluent as long as the handler's signals are consistent.

If, on the other hand, the new behavior is for a specific purpose, such as loading onto a trailer or trotting through a tunnel for Horse Agility, we have to set up special training opportunities to allow the horse to become fluent.

Thin-slicing* the many skills required for trailer-loading leads to fluency.

In my experience, if we train a new behavior to the point of fluency, the horse tends to remember it forever.

If a behavior is unreliable, it was not originally taught to the point of fluency.

After my horse became fluent with backing between two rails on the ground, I did not have to teach that obstacle again every time it was part of a Horse Agility course.

For specific tasks like backing between rails, fluency is a result of clear, consistent signals and frequent, short practices.

Generalization

Once the horse understands a new task or a new skill, it is important to take it out into the world. Through generalization, the horse gains further fluency with a task.

Generalization includes:
1. Asking for the behavior in different places but still at home.
2. Using different props.
3. Working at different times of the day.
4. Asking for the behavior away from home.
5. Working with unusual distractions.

6. Working at a different gait.
7. Handler using a different body orientation.
8. Fading out a signal and replacing it with a new one.
9. Moving to occasional click&treat once the horse knows the task well, rather than each time we ask for the behavior.
10. Working with a different handler (who uses the same signals).

Generalization helps the horse put the new learning into his long-term memory. Each time we quietly repeat the task, we help build the horse's confidence. If the horse is unable to do the task in a specific situation or context, it gives us vital information about where we are in our Education Program* with this horse for this task.

Notes:

Here we are generalizing 'target your knee to my hand' by standing on a balance beam. We don't use the balance beam often, so as with most generalizations, I make a special effort to set it up.

Maintenance

As already mentioned under *Fluency*, some behaviors become and remain fluent because we use them a lot, for example, putting on and taking off a halter or cleaning out the feet every day.

Other behaviors are specialized, and we have to create a plan to refresh and use them occasionally so that they stay in our repertoire. Vet procedures usually come into this category.

If we teach our horse to flex toward the prick of a toothpick, so his muscles are loose rather than taut, we need to do such needle simulations on a regular basis. Likewise, if we want the horse to be confident with a worming tube, we can practice with applesauce as frequently as we like.

Hoof trimming, whether we do it ourselves or hire someone, can cause anxiety for a horse if it suddenly happens out of the blue. It's much easier for us and the horse if we pick up feet regularly and move the feet into trimming positions to make it a normal request. We can also introduce the horse to a variety of different people who are allowed to touch him and handle his legs and feet.

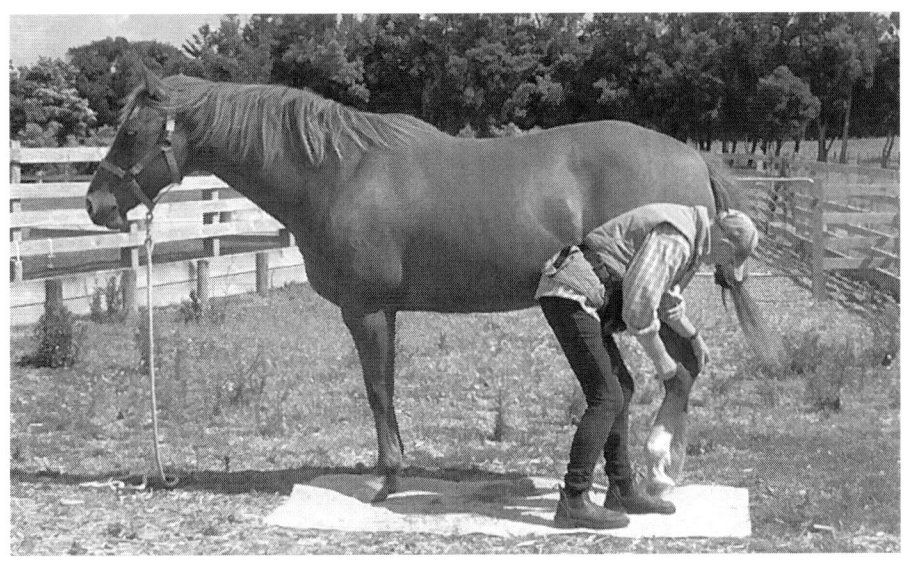

If we regularly clean and check our horse's feet, the co-operative behaviors will easily be maintained. If we depend on someone else to occasionally see to the feet, it will be problematic for the horse.

We must balance the need to build confidence at each tiny step with the need to move on when we should, so the horse doesn't get bored. It's never easy to walk the fine line between going too fast and going too slowly.

Basics of Effective Clicker Training

The information that follows appears in some of my other books. Parts have been revised and expanded.

Materials: Gear Checklist

1. A **training venue** where the horse feels comfortable. Ideally, his herd buddies are in view but not able to interfere.
2. The horse behind a **safe barrier**. This could be a non-wire fence or a gate or a stall guard. Or you could make a small pen for yourself in the horse's paddock.

Protected Contact*: When starting a horse with clicker training, it's wise to use protected contact, which just means keeping a barrier between you and the horse until you have established good table manners. Protected contact allows you to step out of reach if the horse becomes over-enthusiastic. Some horses also feel safer if the person is on the other side of a barrier.

Protected Contact: If we want to work in the horse's paddock or any other large space, we can build a little pen for ourselves. In this picture, I'm using a small plastic bottle for a target. Boots is familiar with electric fences and not worried about working across them when they are turned off. She checks them out with her whiskers. Some horses may be more relaxed if other materials are used as a barrier.

Sometimes the only safe option is to tie the horse up as in the next photo.

Notes:

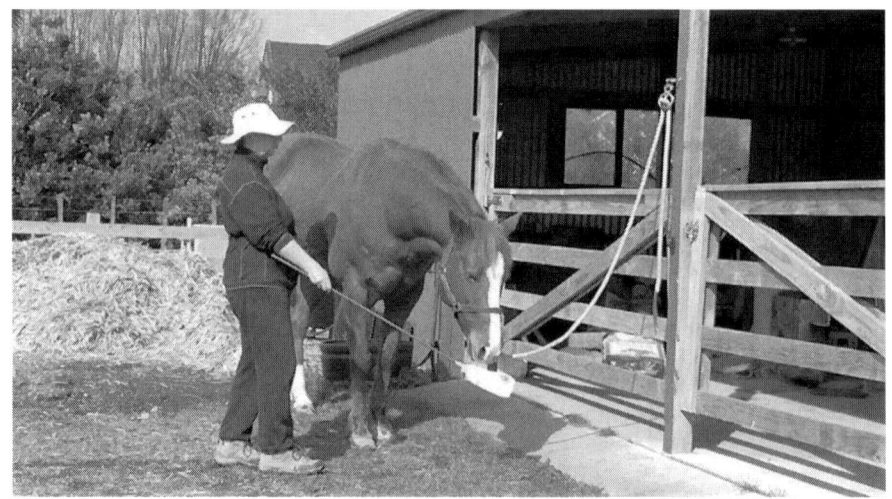

<u>Safety</u>: *In some situations, our only safe option is to have the horse tied up. Tying up with a wide halter is safer than tying with a rope halter in case something causes the horse to pull back. We're also using a Blocker Tie Ring. If the horse pulls back, there will be friction on the rope, but the rope can pull free completely, so the horse's whole weight won't impact the sensitive neck vertebrae.*

You can find out more about the Blocker tie ring at: http://blockerranch.com/.

If the horse is tied up, make sure that he can relax when he is tied. Check that there is enough slack in the rope to allow the horse to move his head freely to touch your target.

However, if the horse is tied up for any other purpose, make sure he is tied much shorter; about three feet or a meter of rope for an average-sized horse.

Protected contact* allows you to stay safe if the horse becomes overly keen or excited about the idea of earning a tasty treat. You won't know how he will react until you have your first few sessions.

3. Decide on your **marker sound**; organize a mechanical clicker if you intend to use one. Having it on a cord around your neck or wrist means you can let go of it when you need to use your hand. But it also means

you must put it back in your hand before you want to use it again so that the timing* of your click is accurate.

I often use a mechanical clicker to teach something new, but most of the time I use a tongue click*. If you can't make a clear tongue click, a special short (one syllable) clear word or sound (not used any other time) works just as well. For simplicity in these notes, I'll use the word 'click' to refer to whatever marker sound you decide to use.

Some horses relate the noise of a mechanical box clicker to the sound of an electric fence zap, in which case you will need to rethink what you will use for a marker sound. There are styles of clickers which give a softer sound, or perhaps use a ball point pen that clicks. The key is to keep the marker sound as unique and consistent as possible.

4. You need a **pouch or pocket** that easily lets your hand slip in and out. One of my favourites is a hoodie-style sweatshirt with a continuous front pocket that allows me easy access to the treats with either hand. Often, I use a bum bag (fanny pack) type pouch.

5. The **treats**: people use tiny portions of carrot, apple, celery, grain, horse nuts, hay cubes, cereal, crackers, dry bread, rice cakes, popped popcorn, nuts, — anything your horse likes. Individual pieces are often easier to manage than loose grain. Casual experimentation lets you find out which treats your horse likes.

My horse loves peppermints, so we use these for very special occasions like a superb response when we are learning something new. Often, I have a variety of treats. Apple pieces score higher with my horse than carrot pieces.

If you want to conduct a more refined experiment, set out a row of dishes with different treats. Set them out in the same order over several sessions and take note of which container the horse approaches first, second, and so on.

Some horses are not keen on 'foreign foods' at first. Freshly picked grass, chaff or hay can sometimes be the right treat to start with.

<u>Treats</u>: *It doesn't take long to get into the habit of getting the treats ready before heading out to our horse.*

6. You can **count out a specific number of treats** for a short training session or just have an abundant treat supply at hand. Running out of treats during a session is not helpful for the horse. I usually have spare horse pellets handy in a sealed container in case I need more.

7. You need a **hand-held target*** to teach the horse that he must *physically do something* (e.g. touch his nose to the target) to earn the click&treat. It's easiest to start with a target on a stick. A plastic drink bottle or milk bottle taped to a stick makes a safe, lightweight target. We can later hang plastic bottles around our training area as destinations where a click&treat will be earned.

If the horse is nervous about sticks due to past experiences, a plastic bottle by itself, as in the photo coming up, may be a better way to start. People variously use cones, fly swatters, telescopic dusters or tennis balls attached to the end of a light stick. Some people simply hold out their arm with their closed fist as the target.

8. Ensure that the horse is **not hungry**. We want the horse to be interested, but not over-excited by the idea of special food coming his way. On the other hand, if the horse seems disinterested in taking treats, try introducing the idea of the click&treat when he is a *little bit* hungry.

9. If your horse is on restricted calories, ensure that his treats count as part of his daily total.

Two Extra Points to Consider

1. If the horse is wary about a new object like a target on a stick or a plastic bottle, I like to walk away backwards with the object (or have a helper walk away backwards with it while the horse and I follow together), and encourage the horse to follow at his own pace until he makes up his own mind that it is okay to put his nose near or on the new item.

   Horses tend to follow things moving away and retreat from things moving toward them. *#93 HorseGym with Boots* demonstrates this idea while getting the horse used to a spray bottle.

   #21 HorseGym with Boots looks at the same idea.

2. If you click by mistake, it's best to deliver the treat anyway. At this point you are training to give meaning to the click, so this is important. We want *the click and the treat* to belong together in the horse's mind. If you click by mistake more than once or twice, go back to practicing your click&treat mechanics with a person standing in for the horse.

Method:

Giving Meaning to the Click

When you introduce the click (or your chosen sound/word) to the horse, it obviously doesn't mean anything at the beginning. We must go through a process that connects the click to the treat that follows it. This is sometimes called 'charging the clicker*'.

My preference is to have the horse do something specific like touching his nose to a target object. The moment his nose (or whisker) touches the object, I click, move the object out of sight behind me so it is out of play, reach for the treat and deliver the treat.

Other clicker trainers 'charge the clicker' by waiting for the horse to turn his head away from the food source and clicking for the 'head away' movement and for keeping the head facing forward away from the handler who is standing beside the horse's neck or shoulder.

My feeling is that turning and keeping the nose away is a rather non-specific thing for the horse to do, as there is no 'destination' in it for the horse. I prefer to teach the 'head away' habit of politeness around food after the horse has already made the click and treat connection using a hand-held target.

Another way to 'charge the clicker' is by standing beside the horse, clicking and giving a treat after each click. This method helps horses who have never learned to take food from a person's hand. Once the horse shows he's made the connection between the click and the food appearing, we quickly move on to having the horse touch a target or move his head away to earn the click&treat.

As mentioned earlier, if your horse seems startled by the sound of a loud box clicker, there are other styles of clicker that are softer, or you could use the click of a retractable ball point pen to introduce the sound. Or begin right away with a tongue click or a specific word or sound. As already mentioned, some horses think the clicker sound is the click of an electric fence experience, so using a unique word, sound or tongue click may again be the way to go.

You can put the clicker on a string around your neck or on a string around your wrist to free your hands as necessary, but sometimes this interferes with good timing*.

Practice with a Person

It's ideal (perhaps even essential) to learn the *process* of when/how to click and how to deliver the treat with a person standing in for the horse. The more adept we are with the mechanics of treat delivery before heading out to the horse, the more our horse will buy into our confidence that we know what we are doing.

As we practice with another person, we start to put the mechanics of treat delivery into our muscle memory. Then, when we start with the horse, we can focus more clearly on the horse and the consistency of our actions.

Simulations: Learning the mechanics of the process with another person standing in for the horse means that the horse doesn't have to put up with all our fumbling as we work out how to organize our bodies.

Simulation with a Person

We must get our head around how to carry out the click&treat routine smoothly and put the sequence of events into our muscle memory (see *Key Stages of New Learning* earlier in this Chapter). If we are familiar and confident with what we are doing, the horse will buy into our confidence.

Have your hand ready on the clicker (if using a clicker).

1. Present the target a little bit away from the person, so he or she has to reach toward it slightly, to touch it.
2. *Wait* for the person to touch the target with their hand (be patient).
3. The instant they touch it, click or say your chosen word or sound.
4. Lower the target down and behind your body to take it out of play.
5. Reach into your pocket/pouch for the treat (maybe use coins or bits of cardboard or mini chocolates).
6. Extend your arm fully to deliver the treat.
7. Stretch your treat hand out flat so it is like a dinner plate with the treat on it.
8. Keep your arm and flat hand firm, so your pretend horse can't push it down as he takes the treat.
9. When your pretend horse has taken the treat, relax and pause briefly, then begin again with step one (hand on clicker, present target).
10. *Ignore* any unwanted behavior as much as possible.
11. Turn a shoulder or move your body/pouch out of reach if the person pretending to be your horse tries to mug you for a treat. Your pretend horse must learn that he or she earns the click&treat only by touching the target. If your 'pretend horse' is strongly invasive, put a barrier between you.
12. Multiple short sessions (up to three minutes long) at different times during the day allow your brain and your muscle memory to absorb the technique, especially the finer points of timing.

13. If your helper is willing, let him/her be the teacher and you take a turn being the horse. Playing with 'being the horse' is often a huge eye-opener. The 'horse' is not allowed to ask questions or make comments.

With the Horse

A: Touching a Target to Earn a Click&treat

The *goal behavior* we are working toward is a horse who willingly moves to follow a target so he can put his nose on it to earn a click&treat. But there are a series of steps (slices*) to reach that goal.

First Session
1. Count 20 or more treats into your pocket/pouch. Have a few spares handy in case you want to finish the session by putting a handful of treats into the horse's food bucket (or on the grass) as an *end of session* routine. If you are using a clicker, have your hand on it ready to use at the right moment.
2. Bring the target from behind your body and quietly hold it out near his nose, but don't *thrust* it at him.
3. *Wait* until he touches even a whisker to it - *click* and *move the target* out of sight behind you. Moving the target out of sight will encourage his attention to the target when you present it again for the next repeat.
4. As you move the target behind you, simultaneously *reach for the treat* and deliver it away from your body by holding your hand out straight and rotating your shoulder to create a solid platform with your totally flat hand. **Never reach for a treat before you click**. It is an easy habit to get into.

Be scrupulous about always reaching for the treat after the click. If you sometimes reach for the treat before you click, the horse will begin to watch for your hand moving to the treat source rather than keep his whole attention on what you want him to do to earn the click&treat.

Occasionally you may want to teach something specific where it works best to have one or more treats already in your hand, so you are able to deliver a treat immediately after the click. But this 'pre-loading' is an exception to use on rare occasions.

To pre-load a treat into your hand, do it quickly while the horse's attention is still on chewing his previous treat.

Treat Delivery: Deliver the treat with a flat hand and an outstretched arm so your body is well away from the horse. After the click, move the target out of sight behind you to 'take it out of play' so it will be obvious to the horse when you present it again for the next repeat. If the horse pushes down on your hand, push upward with equal energy so your hand remains stable in one position.

    5. If using a mechanical clicker, put your hand on it ready to click.

6. Hold out the target again. In your early sessions, present the target in roughly the same place so it remains easy for the horse to touch it. At some point, you will see that he really *gets* the connection between touching the target, the click, and the treat.

7. Repeat until you've used about 20 treats or worked for about three minutes. Ignore unwanted behavior. Ensure that you stop after a good response. As mentioned earlier, a few treats in a feed dish or on the grass is a nice way to let the horse know that one of your mini-sessions is finished. Put the target away out of sight.

8. Lots of mini-sessions (about 20 treats or three minutes) work well. You can do other things with the horse (or chores) between the mini clicker training sessions.

9. Keep all your 'targeting criteria*' the same until you get 10/10 confident repeats in a row for at least three consecutive mini-sessions.

By targeting criteria, I mean:

- Where you train.
- Where you stand in relation to the horse.
- How and where you present the target.

Create a consistent 'end of session' routine that lets the horse know that the clicker training session is finished for now. When I stop, I use a voice signal, "All gone", along with a large gesture signal made by swinging my arms back and forth across each other at waist level several times. As already mentioned, a handful of treats in a food dish or on the grass is a good way to signal that we're finished for now.

We can also use a favorite short activity to mark that the session is about to end.

Part D coming up, outlines how to make the target more interesting once the horse is totally ho-hum and consistent with touching his nose to the target when you hold it out near him.

The clip called *Clicker 1 with Smoky* in my *Starting Clicker Training* playlist illustrates the process of teaching the horse the connection between touching the target, the click, and the treat.

B. Lunging for the Treat

Some horses are always polite, others not so.

1. Be safe. Organize a barrier between you and the horse so you can move back out of range if he gets excited about the idea of food rewards. Depending on the horse and your expertise, you may not need the barrier for long, or you may need it for quite a while.

    If your horse is energetic, you can use up some of the energy by setting up a roomy reverse round pen and teach the horse to follow your target as you walk or jog along.

    A reverse round pen is one where the handler stays inside the pen and the horse moves around the outside of it. Or you can do the same on the other side of an existing fence. For this, you may want to click for the actual movement, rather than catching up with the target.

2. Make sure that the horse is **not hungry**. We want the horse interested in clicker work, but not over-excited or aroused by the thought of food titbits. In other words, make sure he has ample access to grazing or hay before you start a clicker training session.

3. Check out your **food delivery** method.

    a) Does it take too long to get your hand into and out of your pocket or pouch? Can you find easier pockets or a more open pouch?

    b) Do you move your hand toward your treats *before* you've clicked? This can cause problems because the horse will be watching your hand rather than focusing on what you are teaching.

4. Be sure to only feed treats if they have been earned **and** *you have clicked*. Ask the horse to do something before giving a treat, either have him touch a target or take a step or two backwards; click for the action and deliver the treat.

5. Avoid feeding treats by hand unless you have asked for a behavior and clicked for it. When not clicker training, put treats in a feed dish or on the grass.

6. Often, we can influence the horse's position by holding our treat-delivery hand where we want the horse's head to be rather than where he has stuck his nose.

In the beginning, we ideally want him to have his head straight to retrieve the treat. If he is over-eager, it can help to hold the treat toward his chest, so he moves back to receive it. This is the clearest way to let the horse know that lunging at your hand for the treat won't benefit him. It also begins to build the habit of stepping back when you shift your weight toward him, as in the photo below. It's a great way to begin teaching the 'back' voice and body language signal.

<u>Stepping Back for Treat Retrieval</u>: Boots reached across the gate to put her nose on the target. I'm holding my hand with the treat toward her chest to encourage her to take a step back to retrieve it from my hand.

My target in the photo on page 37 is the fly swatter behind my back. I'm holding the clicker in the same hand as the target.

7. In some cases, it can help to have a halter on the horse, so we can take hold of the side of the halter after the click, giving us some control of where the horse puts his mouth. Part C: 'Developing Good Table Manners', is coming up shortly.

8. It can help to run your closed treat hand down the horse's nose from above, asking him to target your fist before you open your hand right under his lips, so he can retrieve the treat.

   As you open your hand, use a bit of upward pressure to stop the horse pushing your hand down. If your hand does not stay firm, it can cause a horse to get anxious about where his treat is and cause him to push down harder or become grabby.

9. It may also work to bring your fist (closed around the treat) up under his chin and have him target your fist before you flatten your hand (and apply upward pressure) so he can retrieve the treat. Often one of these little intervening steps can help build the habit of polite treat-taking.

10. Another approach is to put the treat in a container which you present to the horse after each click. It can either be a food bucket in the horse's pen, into which you toss the treat, or a flat dish you hold out for the horse to retrieve the treat, then remove again. Some boarding facilities have a ban on hand feeding, which would be a little hurdle to overcome.

11. A bit of experimentation will determine what works best with a specific horse.

12. If the horse is overly-keen, try using treats that he doesn't consider quite so yummy and be sure he's had ample time to graze or eat hay before the session.

13. With consistency and patience on the handler's part, over-enthusiastic treat-taking usually improves once:
    a) The horse understands that a click only follows when he carries out a request you have made.
    b) A treat always follows the click.

    He'll learn that a treat will only follow if there has been a click first. That is why we must be totally consistent with when and how we click&treat.

14. The horse's character type and current emotional state will influence how he takes the treat. If a horse who usually takes the treat softly becomes grabbier, he is giving us information to take on board.

    Alternately, a horse who starts out grabby may over many sessions become relaxed about retrieving his treat, once he understands how the system works.

15. Prompt, cleanly-executed treat delivery is always important. If things are not going smoothly, the first things to check are inconsistency and sloppy treat delivery. It helps to video what is happening, so you can look closely at your body position, orientation, timing* and treat delivery.

Check for:

   a) Timing of your click to the action you want.
   b) Smoothness getting the treat out of pocket or pouch.
   c) How promptly you present the treat to the horse.
   d) How you hold out the treat to the horse and how firm your hand is, so the horse doesn't push it down.

C. Developing Good Table Manners

A video clip called *Table Manners for Clicker Training* in my *Starting Clicker Training* playlist illustrates how we can use the timing of the click to improve politeness around treat retrieval. The clip shows Smoky, early in his clicker training education, with Zoë who had never done it before.

The method shown on the clip can be improved by not waiting so long to click&treat again. When we begin teaching a horse about keeping his head facing forward rather than toward us, we want to click&treat the moments when the horse *remains* facing forward, as well as the moments when he turns his head away from the food source.

In some parts of the clip we waited for Smoky to turn toward Zoë and then turn away again, before she clicked. Doing this runs the risk of having the horse think that turning toward the handler first is part of what we want him to do. In this exercise, we also want to click&treat *the act* of the horse *keeping* his head facing forward.

It's hard to overstate the importance of having a way to let the horse know when we just want him to stand beside us quietly. We can use body language to let the horse know that all we want is to stand together in a relaxed manner.

Stand with one or both hands held flat across your belly button, and your energy as close to zero (deflated) as possible, breathing quietly. Relax your hips. If you do this consistently, the horse will soon recognize this posture as your 'neutral' signal when you have zero intent* and all you want is for him to stay quietly parked. Chapter Three looks at this in detail.

The horse will learn that a treat only follows if there has been a click first. That is why we must be totally consistent with when and how we click&treat.

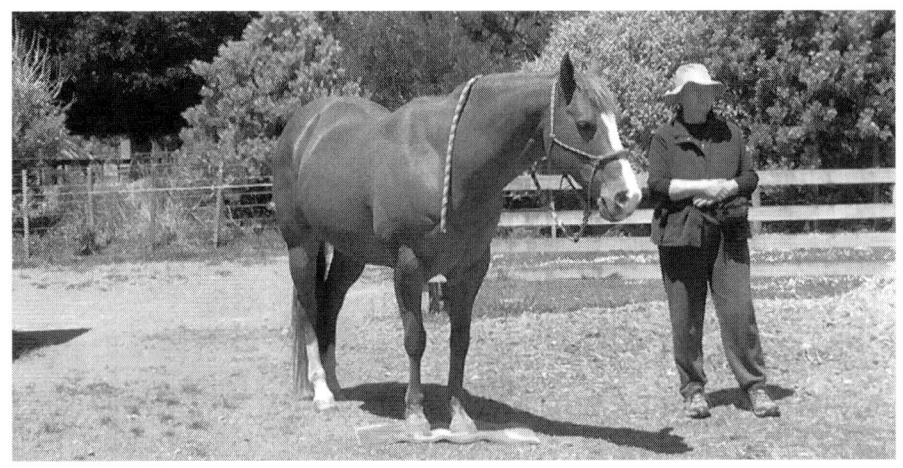

My body language is at 'zero intent*'. My stance and hands lying quietly on my belly tell Boots that the task is to stand quietly. One knee is cocked into 'resting position'. My focus is soft and away from the horse.

To develop good table manners while we stand beside the horse's neck or shoulder, we click&treat for:

- The horse *turning* his head away from us into the 'straight forward' position.
- The horse *keeping* his head straight, away from us.
- The horse keeping his head straight *for longer*, building up duration one second at a time.

Be sure to teach good table manners standing on either side of the horse as well as facing the horse. It's usually best to begin the table manners training in protected contact, i.e. standing on the other side of a fence, gate, or stall guard.

Or we could have the horse tied up. When that is going well, and you feel safe, change to standing with the horse.

It may take lots of very short sessions before the horse is able to relax into the 'head forward' position while we stand with zero intent* beside his shoulder. I find that we practice this skill a little bit almost every time we work together.

As mentioned earlier, I prefer to *introduce* the idea of click&treat by asking the horse to do something more specific such as touch his nose to a target object. Whether or not we are using protected contact in the form of a fence or gate, it's easier to introduce the target if we stand facing the horse.

When the horse is tied up, it may be easier to stand beside the horse to present the target.

Maintaining politeness around food is *always* part of the clicker training equation. It's good to teach food manners standing shoulder-to-shoulder with the horse as soon as the horse has made the connection between the click and the treat.

Hand Feeding at Other Times

It's important not to hand feed the horse unless we have asked for something specific which we can click&treat. If we randomly hand feed when we are not clicker training, the horse will be confused, and problems can arise. As with everything, it is up to us to be clear and consistent all the time. If we visit the horse or check up on him and want to give him a treat, we can put it in a feed bin or on the grass.

D: Targeting: next sessions

#2 HorseGym with Boots shows the process in action. I would improve the technique shown in the first part of the clip by putting the target down behind me, rather than over my shoulder, and standing rather than sitting.

Also, not all horses are comfortable working across electric fencing tape, even if it is not electrified. My horses don't have a problem with it, but other horses might.

1. Once the horse is confidently touching the target held near his nose and seldom loses focus, gradually change the position of the target to make it more challenging. Choose *one* of: higher, lower, to the right, to the left. Teach him each of these one at a time. Each change you make can be a big deal for a horse.

2. Once he reliably moves his neck to touch the target willingly and with interest, ask him to move his whole body a step to the right or the left in order to reach it.

3. When he readily moves one step to touch the target, gradually ask for more steps one at a time. You can still be on the other side of a barrier while you teach this.

4. When you begin to ask the horse to walk along while you move holding the target in front of him, click&treat for the moving along with you, rather than when he 'catches' the target.

   We don't want to turn it into a chasing game. Click for the walking along, and remove the target after you click, while presenting the treat. Then bring the target forward again and walk on. Gradually ask for more and more steps before you click&treat.

5. Whenever you change what you are asking, begin by clicking for even the smallest hint that the horse is beginning to understand what you want. Then gradually withhold the click to get a little more of what you want.

6. When the horse gets confused, *always backtrack* to the place where he can be continuously successful again. This is the key to rapid progress and preserving the horse's desire to keep trying. If he gives up because it's too hard or too confusing, you have lost his willingness.

7. Stop each training segment on a high. Horses think about these things between sessions. Stopping on a good note maintains his motivation to do it again next time. Resist checking to see if the horse can do it again right away.

8. A training segment with clicker work is usually quite short. Between the training segments, we can do chores or other things with the horse.

   Short training segments, repeated often, are the most efficient way to put new learning into long-term memory. Trust that he'll remember. Clicker training gives him an excellent reason to want to remember.

9. When you feel safe, work without the barrier.
10. Get creative to build the horse's confidence until he'll happily follow the target toward, over, between, into and around things.

Working with markers rather than a barrier: We've set up a circle of markers to act as a 'reverse round pen'. Boots is walking around the markers, following Bridget's target. First, Bridget and Boots will stop at each marker for a click&treat. Then they'll stop at every second or third marker and eventually they will walk full circuits around the markers before a click&treat.

It pays to remember that the *process* of teaching does not look like the finished product.

Targets in New Situations: Boots is following the target over the obstacle. The target is a milk bottle taped to a plastic tomato stake.

E. Capturing and Free-Shaping Behaviors

Clicker training can work with reward reinforcement* alone. We quietly, unobtrusively observe, waiting for the horse to do something we want to encourage, and click the exact moment the desired action happens, followed by a treat. In this way, we can 'capture*' a complete behavior.

If we watch the horse's ears and click&treat every time they come forward, we can increase the probability of this behavior -- one that the horse offers naturally. This, however, is controversial because some trainers don't like the idea of interfering with the horse's natural ear expression.

Sometimes capturing and free-shaping* are closely interlinked. When we first ask the horse to touch his nose to a target to earn a click&treat, we capture the targeting behavior. We've captured a behavior that the horse offers naturally due to his innate curiosity. Our behavior of holding out the target, has drawn his attention to the target.

With some types of free-shaping, we use our behavior to influence the horse's behavior. To show the horse that mugging won't work, we quietly wait with zero intent* for the horse to turn his head away from us (and our treat bag or pocket). When we click&treat for the turning away, or keeping the nose away, we are in the process of 'free-shaping' that behavior. The horse can choose to mug* us or face forward. If he is at liberty, he can also choose to walk away. Our behavior (standing quietly with zero intent*) influences the horse's behavior. The treat is only forthcoming if he stays around and keeps his nose away from us.

Another example: we can sit and watch and click&treat each time the horse lowers his head, even just a little bit. Once he's made the connection and drops his head reliably, we can put a signal (either a gesture or a word or both) on the action of lowering the head. Once the signal is established, we can ask him to lower his head whenever we like. Three clips called *Head Lowering* in my *Free-Shaping Examples* playlist illustrate the process.

Once the horse responds correctly to our signal most of the time, we have created a reliable response. Repeated click&treat has built a strong history of reinforcement for that task. We have established the habit of responding to a specific signal through the process of noting something the horse does naturally and marking it with click&treat.

Boots quickly learned to offer a simple bow after I noticed she regularly stretched her front legs forward after getting up from a sleep. I managed to 'capture' the moment with a click&treat three days in a row, and after that she began to offer the bow from standing in order to earn the reward. I 'captured' the behavior by marking it and she realized that she could influence my behavior (deliver a click&treat) by bowing.

We captured the 'bow' by marking, with a click&treat, her habit of stretching after getting up from a nap. Now she volunteers it daily because it is sure to earn a click&treat every time she does it.

If we feed our horse at about the same time every day, he probably comes over expecting to be fed whenever he sees us at a certain time. We have free-shaped a reliable response because our arrival at that time has been rewarded day after day. It has become a habit.

The photo below shows Boots bringing over her feed dish at dinner time. This behavior is the result of a long process of free-shaping. We can't force a horse to pick up an object and carry it. Some horses enjoy picking things up and playing with them. Others, like Boots, can learn it via many free-shaping sessions.

There are more examples in my *Free-Shaping Examples* playlist.

Horses immediately pick up if we are unsure about what we are doing.

Free-shaping example: To learn this, we gradually moved our click point* from sniffing the bucket, to putting lips on the side of the bucket, to picking up the bucket, to walking while holding the bucket. But first, we had to separately shape learning to carry a stick while out walking together. Even though she willingly picked things up, walking while holding something in her mouth was a new concept for Boots.

F. Guided Shaping

If we want to teach the horse a skill that is not part of naturally-offered behavior, we can give him hints to encourage him to do something specific to earn a click&treat. For example:

- Gentle pressure on the chest to suggest a step back; click&treat.

- Drawing the horse around a corner with our energy; click&treat.

- Asking the horse to yield his shoulder to make a counter-turn away from us; click&treat.

- Walking forward to follow a target can morph into gentle pressure on a halter, or neck rope; click&treat.

  Targets can be helpful to initiate a behavior, but we usually want to phase them out. We introduce the new signal, then use the old signal and the horse will soon transfer his attention to the new signal, at which point we can phase out the old signal.

- Gentle touch on a leg to lift it up; click&treat.

Once the horse easily offers a new behavior when we suggest it, we can add a distinct voice signal to the touch or gesture. With time and practice, the touch and gesture signals can become tiny and sophisticated.

The more often we ask the horse to repeat a behavior to earn a click&treat, the more it will become firmly established in his deep memory. Boots now routinely picks up her bucket and brings it to the shed at feeding time.

G. Counter Conditioning

Counter conditioning* is a form of 'guided shaping*'. It is a behavioral term for gradually getting a horse used to something which is not part of a horse's natural life. We pair a desired consequence (e.g. click&treat) with something that causes natural anxiety. Habituation*, desensitization and 'building confidence' are all terms used to describe the same objective, which is a horse who can stay relatively relaxed in a variety of situations.

For example:

- Confidence with humans nearby.
- Confidence with human touch.
- Accepting a halter put on.
- Confidence with things like tarps and umbrellas.
- Accepting being shut into a truck or trailer.

- Accepting the commotion of venues such as showgrounds, clinics.
- Accepting being left in a stall.
- Accepting horse buddies going out of sight.
- Accepting leaving home without his buddies.
- Accepting being washed with a hose.
- Accepting foot care routines.
- Accepting a saddle or harness on his body.
- Accepting the pressure of a girth.
- Accepting the weight of a rider.
- Accepting road traffic.
- Becoming comfortable with new riding or walking places.

We have to remember that these things are not part of a horse's natural life. All animals have the cognitive (thinking) abilities necessary to survive in their natural environment. In the case of horses, their natural environment requires group membership, 24/7 access to forage, extensive freedom of movement while grazing or seeking water and constant vigilance for predators and other dangers. As well, mares will be busy raising foals.

The fact that many horses can adapt so well to the weird things people do to them and with them is truly amazing. Nothing in their natural life prepares them for the demands of domestic life.

Counter conditioning is a process of splitting (slicing) big expectations into small enough pieces (slices) so we can gradually build the horse's confidence with each slice in turn. The life of domestic horses is full of situations that activate their fear and flight responses.

Clicker training makes it easier for us to explain to the horse that this strange new thing or place is not going to harm you; in fact, it can earn you a treat.

For example, to get a horse comfortable with vehicles moving past, we can make the approach of a vehicle a click point*. The vehicle passing us can be another click point. The ideal place to start such training is with a controlled situation where a friend is driving the car or riding the bicycle.

One of my horse's paddocks abuts a narrow lane bringing fresh vegetables to a packing house. Huge trucks with trailers drive past several times day and night. She is now so used to them she barely looks up as they trundle past a few yards away. Frequent exposure has habituated* her to big rigs. She has become desensitized to them.

If we daily feed our horse his regular special meal in his trailer, we are counter conditioning his tendency to be anxious about small enclosed spaces.

If we want our horse relaxed about wearing a saddle, we can put it on, feed him his special meal, then unsaddle him. Counter conditioning means putting a positive spin on something that is not part of normal wild horse life.

Once the saddling is smooth, we can continue the counter conditioning by taking the saddled horse for a walk to nice grazing or a pile of hay strategically placed. To habituate the horse further, we do ground work with him wearing his saddle, so he can get used to the feel of it in many situations and at all gaits.

Thin-Slicing to Create Individual Education Programs*

When we observe someone else's horse perform a finished behavior, it's often tempting to try it ourselves by repeating it as we saw it. But that is not how it works.

When we want to teach something new, the first step is to experiment gently to see what the horse can offer already in relation to the new goal behavior we'd like to achieve. This will give us an idea of where our Individual Education Program (IEP)* for this horse needs to start. We want to base our Program on foundation training with which the horse is already confident.

It is also a good way to find any 'training holes' that we need to fill before we enthusiastically head toward setting a new challenge for the horse.

Once we have a starting point, we can begin to write our Plan and IEP by thin-slicing* the overall task.

The first step of thin-slicing is a brainstorm* to dissect our goal behavior into its smallest teachable components. Then we must organize these components or 'slices' into an order that we think will make sense to a horse.

This possible order of slices becomes the basis of our Training Plan*. We then transform a general Training Plan into an Individual Education Program for a specific horse.

The remainder of this book sets out twelve Training Plans. That is as far as I can go. The Individual Education Programs will be created by each individual handler and horse working together.

What makes sense to a particular horse depends on:

- His innate character type.
- His previous life experiences.
- The degree of communication that already exists between the horse and the handler.
- Frequency of the training sessions.
- How comfortable the horse feels in the training environment.
- Effective, creative use of objects and obstacles to make it easier for the horse to understand the handler's intent.

An IEP is always a 'work in progress' and usually we go back and tweak it many times. Sometimes we throw the whole thing out and start again. Each time we work with a horse,

IEP Individual Education Programme.

we get additional feedback* from the horse and from our own reactions and responses.

Thin-slicing* means carefully checking (and re-checking) that the horse is comfortable and confident with each tiny slice of the process before we move on. It pays to remember that the *process* of teaching does not look like the finished product.

We must balance the need to build confidence at each tiny step with the need to move on when we should, so the horse doesn't get bored. It's never easy to walk the fine line between going too fast and going too slowly.

It all becomes easier as experience:

- Gives us a deeper understanding of a particular horse's character type.
- Improves our reading of the nuances of the horse's body language.
- Makes us more aware of our own body language and the messages we are sending.
- Improves our thin-slicing, thus creating better programs for a particular horse.

Successive Approximations

In simple English, this means that we start with what the horse can offer already, and gradually direct and reward each tiny change in the direction of the final behavior we want.

In other words, at the beginning of teaching something new, we release (click&treat) for the slightest approximation of what we want relating to our goal behavior. Each approximation becomes one slice of the overall task.

Each time the horse feels ready, we encourage him to do a tiny bit more to gain the release (click&treat). This whole process of rewarding successive approximations is called 'shaping'* a behavior.

A human example of 'shaping a behavior' is teaching a child to write. We start with holding a pencil and using it to make random marks on paper. At some point the random marks become conscious curves and straight lines.

When the time is right, we introduce writing the letters of the alphabet. Eventually the child can group letters to make words. Words are then arranged into meaningful sentences. Some children go on to write coherent paragraphs, essays, stories, blogs or books.

If the child loses confidence with any of the 'slices' of the process, an element of discomfort can creep in, along with typical avoidance behavior. Not enough practice then results in a poorly shaped skill.

Writing is an interesting human endeavor that starts at two years old and is still in formative stages ten years later.

Another way to look at successive approximations is to think of a sculptor starting with a piece of stone. He works in careful stages until the shape in his mind is visible to the rest of us in the shape of his sculpture.

In the same way, we gradually tease a series of movements (or stillness) out of a horse to yield a complete task. This is a bit harder than shaping stone because horses have minds of their own.

Signals

I like to use the word *signal* rather than *cue* because by definition, a signal means the same to the sender and the receiver. We can give cues right, left and center, but unless we've carefully taught the horse what we mean, the horse will remain bemused or confused.

Building coherent signals is what training is all about. Most signals arise naturally from what is being taught.

It helps to decide early on what signals we will use and be totally consistent once we've made the decision after the experimenting stage. Voice signals need to be distinct from each other. The best voice signals are short, clear and not used in other contexts.

For example, my horse knows "whoa" for stopping, so when training long-reining I did not use "haw" for turning left because it sounds too much like "whoa". I used "left" instead.

The horse can only be as soft and responsive as the handler's signals are clear and soft. Our signal releases and rewards need to be intimately responsive to the horse's actions.

Signals can be one of, or any combination of:

- Energy level of your body.
- Your breathing rate.
- Your body orientation.
- Your body language.
- Distinct words or sounds.
- Hand/arm gesture (at first perhaps emphasized with a body extension*).
- Touch.

This is a body language, low energy, low breathing rate gesture greeting signal which emulates horses touching noses when they greet a herd member. We always let the horse close the last little distance to our hand so that the greeting touch is entirely the horse's choice.

My book, *Conversations with Horses, An In-Depth Look at Cues & Signals between Horses & their Handlers*, explores this subject in depth.

#31 - #38 HorseGym with Boots (inclusive) illustrate specific aspects about signals.

Pauses, Dwell Time and Down Time

Pauses and dwell time consist of quiet moments that we build into our sessions to give the horse time to absorb the things we are teaching.

- We can use *pauses* between requests to repeat a movement.

- We can use *pauses* as we move between obstacles or places we want to work.

- We can amplify *pauses* into *dwell time** where we wait a bit longer for the horse to enjoy his treat and relax for a minute or so.

- We communicate *pauses* and *dwell time* to the horse by taking up 'zero intent*' body language. Chapter Three is about getting good with moving into and out of zero intent.

- We can amplify *dwell time* into a few minutes of *down time* if we stop for a spot of grazing or a snooze or grooming (if the horse enjoys grooming — some horses only tolerate it). Sometimes we run out of treats and can give the horse *down time* while we get some more.

- *Down time* can be spent watching another horse's training session, chatting with a friend or spending undemanding time with our horse.

"Down time' enjoying each other's company and a bit of sun.

Horses learn a lot from watching each other. If they grew up with other horses, it's by watching their herd mates that they learned much of what is okay and what should be avoided. I think we often underestimate how much horses (and all birds and mammals) learn by watching what is going on around them.

The more we enrich our horse's daily environment, the more active his mind will be. If we keep a horse or a child mostly in a room by himself with a window looking into a concrete yard, he won't have many skills to deal with the outside world.

Parameters

A parameter is something we decide to keep the same or *constant.*

For example:

Walking on the horse's left side might be a *constant* or parameter you have chosen.

- If you then change to walking on his right side, that is a new parameter.

- If you want to draw the horse around you into a turn, you have changed a parameter.
- If you want to influence the horse to turn away from you, you have changed a parameter.
- When you ask the horse to jog with you rather than walk with you, you have changed a major parameter.
- Walking on an *unfamiliar* road or track is a major change of parameter.
- If you are walking toward a familiar destination mat where he knows he will halt to earn a click&treat, and you ask him to halt before he reaches the mat, you have changed a parameter.
- If you are walking a around a rail lying on the ground and then want to walk across the rail, you are changing a parameter.

When we ask the horse to walk with us in a new environment rather than at home in a familiar area, we have changed a major parameter.

Whenever we change a parameter, it is important that we increase the rate of reinforcement* (i.e. click&treat more often) and work our way forward again until we and the horse are both confident in the new situation, with one click&treat at the end of a task or a series of tasks.

Horses are super observant of all changes, large or small, and can often be 'thrown' by them if we proceed too fast or ask for too much too soon. They also immediately pick up if we are unsure about what we are doing.

As outlined earlier, it's important to have a written Individual Education Program* before we delve into teaching our horse something new. If we can clearly visualize what we are working on, that confidence will be picked up by the horse. He can only be as confident as we are confident.

Summary

Unless we are free-shaping* a task, clicker training (reward reinforcement*) can easily be used in conjunction with release reinforcement*.

When we use both together, the click&treat dynamic:

- Allows the horse to understand much more quickly exactly what we'd like him to do.
- Hooks the horse's attention and allows him to be pro-active in the training session rather than always having to be re-active to the requests of the handler. We have to carefully balance the horse offering trained behaviors with having the behaviors 'on signal' or 'on cue', especially where safety is a factor.
- Adds interest to the horse's interactions with the handler and encourages his motivation and willingness to learn new things.
- Activates the *resource-seeking* part of the horse's brain and keeps him highly motivated to work out what you want — often easily for as long as the treats hold out.

- Encourages the handler to think deeply about how to thin-slice a task and plan an Individual Education Program* before heading out to the horse.
- Encourages the handler to look for desired actions to click&treat rather than focus on mistakes to correct.
- Teaches the handler to reset* tasks when the horse gets confused, rather than 'correct' the horse.

The remainder of the book presents twelve ground skills and a possible way to thin-slice* each one.

Reminder: I can only present Training Plans*. It remains up to each handler to design an Individual Education Program* for each horse in their care.

When the horse gets confused, always backtrack to the place where he can be continuously successful again.

This is the key to rapid progress and preserves the horse's desire to keep trying.

If he gives up because it's too hard or too confusing, you have lost his confidence and his willingness.

Chapter Two

Parking with Duration

INTRODUCTION:

An easy way to begin teaching parking with duration is to use mats as foot targets. Mats can be anything safe for the horse to put his feet on.

For mats I use anything safe for the horse to stand on: pieces of plywood, old bathmats, old saddle blankets, old car mats, rubber door mats, carpet samples or old pieces of carpet.

I've included parking in this book because it is one of the most useful foundation tasks we can teach our horse. By being precise about letting the horse know when we want him to stand still and when we want him to do something else, we add a most useful dimension into our relationship.

Unless horses are resting or scanning the environment to check on their safety status, they seldom stand still. Grazing horses move along one step at a time as they seek out the next bit of forage. They walk purposefully to water or a new grazing area. They move away from perceived danger and toward something that catches their interest. They engage in social interactions.

What horses don't do is stand still when something unusual is happening. We have to educate our horse to be 'actively inactive' for all the things we want to do with him standing still:

- Grooming.
- Foot care.
- Saddling/harnessing/covers on and off
- Mounting and dismounting.
- Vet procedures.
- Being tied up.
- Traveling in a truck or trailer.

None of the above relate to the life of a free-living horse. By teaching parking on a mat with positive reinforcement, we give the horse a reason to plant his feet in one place – a reason that he can understand.

A horse who confidently parks on a mat does not need to be cross-tied. We can avoid having to use such 'straight-jacket', restrictive handling procedures by teaching the horse to love mats.

He learns to love standing on a mat by giving it a strong history of positive reinforcement as well as continuing to practice and reward it regularly. Standing on the mat (and eventually staying there for a while) becomes the horse's idea.

#20 HorseGym with Boots: The Art of Standing Still illustrates.

PREREQUISITES:
- Horse understands the basics of clicker work.
- Handler can time the click/marker sound to the desired action (or in this case, 'inaction' for a specific time).
- Handler can read (or is learning to get better at reading) horse body language to know when the horse is relaxed and when he is not.
- Handler can smoothly change his/her body language from 'intent' to 'no intent'. Chapter Three looks at this in detail.

ENVIRONMENT & MATERIALS:
- A work area where the horse is relaxed and confident.
- Ideally, the horse can see his buddies, but they can't interfere.
- Halter and lead (avoiding pressure on the lead) or work at liberty in a safe, enclosed area.
- For free-shaping the approach to the mat, work at liberty if possible. If you must use a lead, a lightweight one at least 12' long tends to be easier to handle with minimal touch interference on the horse's head.
- One or more mats.

AIMS:
A. To encourage the horse to explore an object and make up his own mind that it is harmless.
B. To encourage the horse to see a mat as a desirable spot because standing on the mat always results in a click&treat.
C. To build duration stayed relaxed standing on a mat.
D. To build duration staying parked <u>without</u> a mat in different places.

#124 HorseGym with Boots illustrates free-shaping mat targets.

October 2017 Park & Wait in the *Obstacle Challenges* playlist illustrates working with 'Parking' in a variety of situations with an emphasis on the handler having a very clear 'no intent' body language.

Chapter Three looks in greater detail at 'Zero Intent' and 'Intent'.

Free-Shaping the Horse's Approach to The Mat

SLICES:

1. Lay out a mat well away from the horse while the horse is watching.
2. Stand back and casually observe the horse's responses. Be careful not to stare directly at him; have a soft, relaxed body language.
3. Click & walk to the horse to deliver the treat if:

    a) he looks at the mat.

    b) he steps toward the mat.

    c) he sniffs the mat.

    d) he touches the mat with a foot.

    e) he paws at the mat, click the moment he stops pawing.

4. Once he has put a nose or foot on the mat and received his click&treat, move the horse away from the mat, then release him again, or move his feet off the mat so you can pick it up and toss it away. You could also use a second mat to toss away from him. Then go back to observing, repeating 3 above.
5. If the horse shows little interest in the mat, put a favored treat on it while he is watching and let him decide what to do.

To encourage the horse to approach a mat we can put a favorite treat on it to encourage his curiosity.

6. If you are working alone, it may be easier to have two mats and as he eats the treat on one mat, you can be putting another treat on the other mat. The mats can be close together at first, then gradually further and further apart.

7. Once the horse loves going to mats due to a strong history of reward reinforcement*, we can use mats as parking spots to help us teach tasks like tying up, grooming, foot care, saddling, vet care and so on.

   I've found that carpet stores are happy to give away their old carpet sample books. They are amused when I tell them why I want them.

Building Duration

#8 HorseGym with Boots Duration on the Mat illustrates;

To build duration, gradually, one second at a time, wait a bit longer before you click&treat.

If the horse moves:

- Don't make him feel wrong. He is letting you know that he can't yet stay there for that long.

- Walk a little circuit together so you end up back at the mat, click& retreat at reaching the mat and wait a shorter time segment that the horse can achieve.
- Try very hard to always click&treat BEFORE the horse feels any need to move.
- You could set up two or more mats and park on each one in turn, adding a bit of movement between asking for duration again.

Slow and steady will get you there. It's better to click well within the horse's capability rather than focus too quickly on lengthening the duration.

Lower-energy horses will find building parking duration easier than high-energy horses. If you have a high-energy horse, work with this task after a higher-energy workout so he is more likely to feel like standing still.

If you are going to tie up your horse or ask him to travel in a vehicle, aim for a few minutes of relaxed parking while you stand or sit near him.

If I want to teach parking duration for longer than 60 seconds, I find it helpful to set up a lane for the horse to stand in (on a mat at first) and I take a chair, so I can sit on the outside of the lane. Lanes or a box shape of ground rails help delineate the parking spot for the horse.

Generalizations

The following video clips outline possible ways to build on the basic Parking task.

#9 HorseGym with Boots: Putting the Mat on Cue.

#10 HorseGym with Boots: Generalizing Mats.

#11 HorseGym with Boots: Mat-athons.

#12 HorseGym with Boots: Chaining Tasks (with mats).

#15 HorseGym with Boots: Parking at a Distance.

#18 HorseGym with Boots: Parking out of Sight.

November 2017 Obstacle Challenge: Mat Madness. This looks at things to do with mats if the horse already knows a lot of stuff.

If I want to work on 'parking' for longer than a minute, I like to set up a 'special place' like a lane and take a chair for me to sit on. If the horse moves, we simply walk a circuit, reset* the task and start timing again. They key is never to ask the horse to wait for longer than he can achieve comfortably before rewarding with a click&treat.

Build the parking duration in one-second intervals. Relaxation is more important than how long the horse can stay there.

It's better to click well within the horse's capability rather than focus too quickly on lengthening the duration.

Notes

Chapter Three

'Zero Intent' and 'Intent'

INTRODUCTION:

One way we can make it easier for our horse to understand what we would like him to do, is to refine our own body language. The horse can only be as precise in his responses as we are precise with our body language.

We want to be as clear as possible when we ask the horse to do something new, and equally clear when we want him to just stand or walk with us in a relaxed manner.

If we reliably assume a distinct stance and put our hands in a certain position to indicate that we don't need anything to happen, the horse soon realizes that our posture is meaningful for him.

'Zero Intent' posture for staying parked: energy drained from my body, hands lying on my bellybutton, hips relaxed, one knee cocked, shoulders down, looking nowhere.

It is a bit like the computer binary system of zero and one. Either we want the horse to stand (or walk with us) in a relaxed manner or we want him to begin moving part of his body or his whole body in a particular way.

'Zero Intent' (sometimes called 'neutral') means that we want the horse to keep on doing what he is doing. On the ground, this might include:

- Standing 'parked'.
- Walking beside us at a steady pace in a relaxed manner.
- Maintaining the gait we have asked for if we are lunging the horse.

We express 'Intent'* with signals we have taught the horse. When we first teach a new task, we can make our intent clearer if we engineer the horse's environment to make the behavior* we want more likely to happen. Once the horse does the desired behavior reliably, we can add voice and gesture signals.

For example. If our intent is to have the horse confidently walk onto a tarp, we can put a favorite treat on the tarp, so it becomes the horse's idea to put his feet on the tarp in order to reach the treat. We are still free-shaping* the behavior of walking onto a tarp, but we are helping it along by setting up an environment that increases the chances of it happening.

Behaviors that start and end with the horse standing parked with us in a relaxed manner are ideal for improving our 'Zero Intent' and 'Intent' body language. For example:

- Touch a hand-held target which we then put behind us 'out of play' as we deliver the treat
- A halt to walk transition followed by a walk to halt transition.
- Backing up from halt.
- Yielding forequarters.
- Yielding hindquarters.
- Head down.

- Picking up a foot.

We begin with zero intent, signal the horse with intent, click&treat when the horse carries out our intent, then return to zero intent.

When we practice this consciously, we remove much of the 'noise' and unnecessary energy or tension we hold in our bodies, which confuses horses because they are extremely sensitive to body language*.

If there is no consistency in our body language, horses tend to regard all of it as meaningless and tune it out.

'Intent': I've lifted my torso, breathed in and am activating my fingers into our signal for Boots to move her shoulder over.

#153 HorseGym with Boots: Zero Intent and Intent illustrates: On the video clip I use 'No Intent' to mean the same as 'zero Intent'. The clip demonstrates a variety of tasks that begin with the 'parked' position.

PREREQUISITES:
- Horse and handler are clicker savvy.

- Horse has learned a few tasks that he can do from a parked position (see Chapters One and Two)
- Handler has practiced awareness of his/her 'zero intent' posture away from the horse. If you can, use another person as a 'sounding board' for your changes in body language. Using a mirror will help. Things to work with for zero intent are:
    1. Energy deflated from body with a deep breath out.
    2. Shoulders relaxed down.
    3. Breathing slow and quiet.
    4. Hands lying quiet on bellybutton.
    5. Hips relaxed.
    6. Maybe one knee cocked.
    7. Eyes soft and away from the horse (e.g. gazing at the ground).
- Then practice coming out of 'zero intent' posture into the body language and gesture signals for the behaviors that you will ask for.

ENVIRONMENT & MATERIALS:
- A work area where the horse is relaxed and confident.
- Horse is not hungry.
- Ideally, the horse can see his buddies, but they can't interfere.
- Halter and lead (avoiding pressure on the lead) or work at liberty in a safe, enclosed area.

AIMS:
A. Handler becomes super-aware of (and consistent with) moving into and out of 'zero intent' body language.

B. Horse becomes super-aware of the difference between 'intent' and 'zero intent' in the handler's body language.

SLICES:

Before you begin, visualize what tasks you will ask the horse to do with your intent signals.

Here are some possibilities:

- Present a hand-held target, then remove it out of sight behind you as you deliver the treat.
- From halt to walk toward a mat destination to halt again (see Chapter Two).
- From halt to back-up to halt again (see Chapters Eight and Nine).
- From halt to move forequarters to halt again.
- From halt to move hindquarters to halt again.
- From halt to target one of: chin, knee, eye, ear, cheek, shoulder to hand (see Chapter Five).

GENERALIZATION:

- The '20-Steps Exercise' in Chapter Six is another context to help become fluid with the 'intent' and 'no intent' dynamic.
- Once the horse stays parked reliably, we can begin to move into different positions around him, taking up the 'zero intent' body language so he easily understands that nothing is required of him except to remain parked. The skill is to maintain our 'zero intent' while we move into different positions around the horse. This video clip demonstrates: *Oct 2017 Park & Wait*:
- Focus on developing 'zero intent' body language when walking with your horse beside you. By walking in a relaxed posture, with a drape (smile) in the lead rope,

breathing evenly, the horse has the opportunity to mirror your 'at ease' demeanour. Just as horses are conscious of any tension we hold in our bodies, so they are conscious when we let go of the tension.
- As we become more aware of our body language, it gets easier and easier to apply our 'zero intent' postures to let the horse know that nothing is required of him at the moment except to stand or walk with us quietly.

On the left, 'no intent'. On the right, I'm using our signal for 'head down'.

The video clips make it much easier to get an overall picture. Practice with visualizing changes from 'zero intent' to 'intent' can be most helpful.

When we consciously become aware of our body language, we can strive to remove much of the 'noise' and unnecessary energy or tension we hold in our bodies.

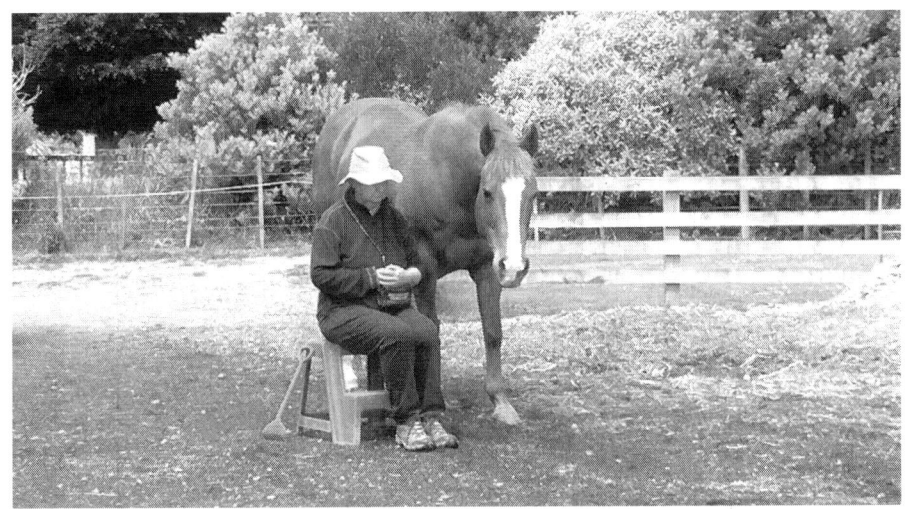

The 'no intent' position sitting down.

Notes:

Notes:

Chapter Four

Seeking the Horse's 'Consent' Signals

INTRODUCTION:

Most of horse training is to teach the horse our signals that he needs to know to keep ourselves and the horse as safe as possible in different situations. If we check human health insurance claims, a fair number are horse-related.

New Zealand, with a population in 2017 of 4.79 million, recorded 7873 people with horse-related injuries. Of these, 2852 fell off a horse. Horse accident insurance claims for 2017 came to $9,669,964.00.

No one knows how many horses have a short life because they don't fit in with the demands of their constrained domestic existence which is, in many cases, completely foreign to a horse's natural lifestyle.

The health insurance figures above suggest that there is room for improvement in human-horse and horse-human communication.

Fortunately, more and more people are becoming aware that the best training fosters two-way communication between person and horse.

Writers such as Sharon Wilsie (*HorseSpeak*) and Rachaël Draasima (*Language Signs & Calming Signals of Horses*) and my book, *Conversations with Horses*, are helping horse people to appreciate just how much information horses impart to us with their body language.

Horses use distinct body language. Sadly, many people are blind to this language or choose to ignore it.

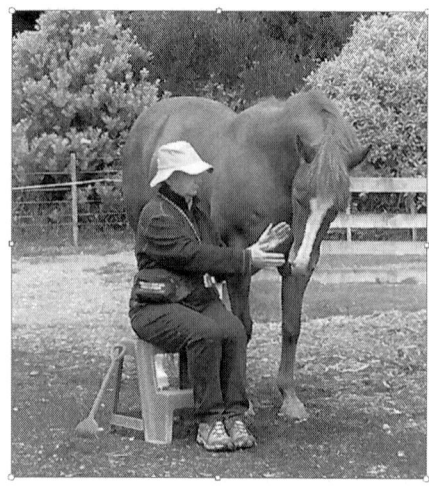 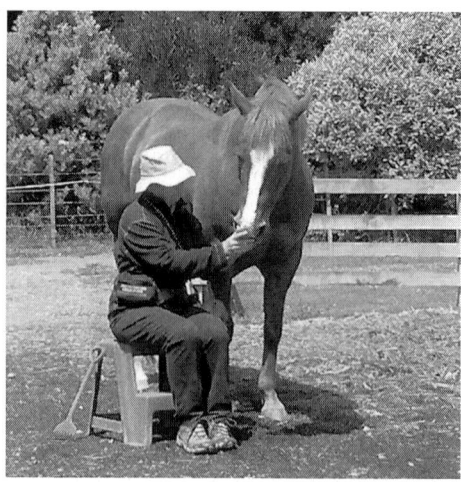

'Okay to Repeat' for Mouth Inspection. <u>Left</u>: I put out my hands, which indicate the task. Boots, who had dropped her head, now lifts it up to place her nose between my hands. <u>Right</u>: She keeps her head in place while I lift her lips to inspect her teeth.

A horse's world view is dictated by the way he senses the environment. His vision, hearing, smell and sense of proximity are different and mostly superior to ours. He has evolved adaptations that allow him to survive in open grassland rife with predators and profound seasonal changes.

Humans have a different history with different selection pressures. We sense our environment differently. With us, verbal language has, on the surface, supplanted body language.

Horses use distinct body language. Sadly, many people are blind to this language or choose to ignore it. The magic is that once we begin to observe and pay attention to what horses are saying, we start to pick up the nuances and get better at tailoring our training to the sensitivities of individual horses.

While there are differences, there are also similarities. Both humans and horses are gregarious*. They live in groups with extensive social interaction between group members. Living in a group means that there is always a balance between competition for the same resources and the need to maintain peaceful relations.

When resources are plentiful, there is minimum competition and maximum peacefulness. When resources are scarce, peacefulness is interrupted by competition as the more assertive group members jockey for the best resources.

Although people don't consider body language as important as spoken language, we still display it clearly. We also react to it subconsciously. Between spouses and close friends, it speaks volumes.

People like scam artists, who prey on other people's susceptibilities, are astute readers of body language, using it to single out their victims. Horses can definitely read our body language, despite the species barrier.

As well as reading each other's body language, horses read the body language of their predators. They know when they are in hunting mode, just passing by, or resting in the vicinity.

Horses are also aware that their own body language sends messages to predators, who look for signs of weakness or lameness. That is why it is often so hard to know if our horse is in pain. They will hide pain and infirmity as much as they possibly can.

What are 'Okay to Repeat' or 'Okay to Proceed' Signals?

'Okay Signals' are initiated by the horse to let us know that they feel okay for us to repeat what we are doing or to carry on with a procedure that involves a variety of things.

When I'm walking on the road with Boots, I've become aware of her need to stop and assess things such as cows moving in the distance, a vehicle in an unusual place or something that has changed in the environment since we last passed by.

If I stop with her and wait, paying attention to what has caught her attention, we are 'on the same page'. I breathe out loudly to show that I'm okay with this thing that has caught our attention and relax into 'zero intent*'.

Eventually Boots will lower her head and bring her attention back to me, which tells me that she has satisfied her need to notice and is ready to walk on.

Once we learn to pause with zero intent* long enough to allow the horse to communicate with us, we can discover ways that individual horses will let us know when they are ready to repeat whatever we are asking, so they can earn another click&treat.

I think many good trainers are already unconsciously aware of these signals, without having given the concept a name. I think that isolating and focusing on this type of horse-initiated signal can open a new vista of training.

It is not hard to recognize horses communicating loudly when they don't want to do something. It is not always easy, however, to know whether not wanting to do something stems from:

- Fear.
- Pain.
- The horse not understanding what we would like him to do.

We have to observe carefully if we want to learn to recognize horses communicating when they are not shouting loudly with their body language. Unless we train ourselves to understand the finer points of their signaling, we miss most of what they are trying to tell us.

Most horse communication is visual. Horses in an established group seem harmonious because a flick of an ear, the tilt of the neck, a single swish of the tail, a certain posture of the body, are all highly meaningful to another horse.

People are usually, understandably, so focused on their own agenda that they miss most of these signals. But we can do better. Since we remove horses from their natural life and make them captive to us, the least we can do is try hard to learn their language and use it to aid two-way communication.

The concept of waiting for a horse to give permission or consent for us to carry on with a task may be a novel idea for some people.

As mentioned earlier, good trainers probably do this subconsciously. They continuously observe the horse's body language to gauge whether the horse is comfortable about proceeding with the training or repeating a specific task. Is it best to pause for a while, do something easy or finish for the day?

Our fondest personal memories are often of things we have successfully initiated and controlled. In the same way, horses respond positively to having control and ownership of what is going to happen next in their lives.

In other words, a sense of control is as reinforcing to horses as it is to people. We steal a great deal of their personal control when we bring them into captivity.

When it becomes the horse's idea to initiate their handler's next action, the horse begins to share 'ownership' of the behavior we are working with. Such a feeling of ownership alleviates the anxiety and tension that arise if the horse is constrained and forced to accept what is being done to him.

Much of what we do with a horse requires him to stand still. As mentioned in Chapter Two, standing still when unusual things are happening is not what evolution found useful for horse survival.

As outlined in Chapter Two, standing still is very much a skill that must be taught and developed.

For many activities, we'll still have to read the horse's overall body language to know if he is okay to proceed with what we are doing. But for some specific tasks, we can incorporate an 'okay to repeat' or an 'okay to proceed' signal from the horse. There are several ways of doing this.

'Okay to Repeat' Using Nose Targets

If a horse has a strong history of positive reinforcement* for staying parked in a relaxed manner with his nose on or near a nose target, we can use his willingness to stay, and touch the target again, as his 'okay to repeat' signal.

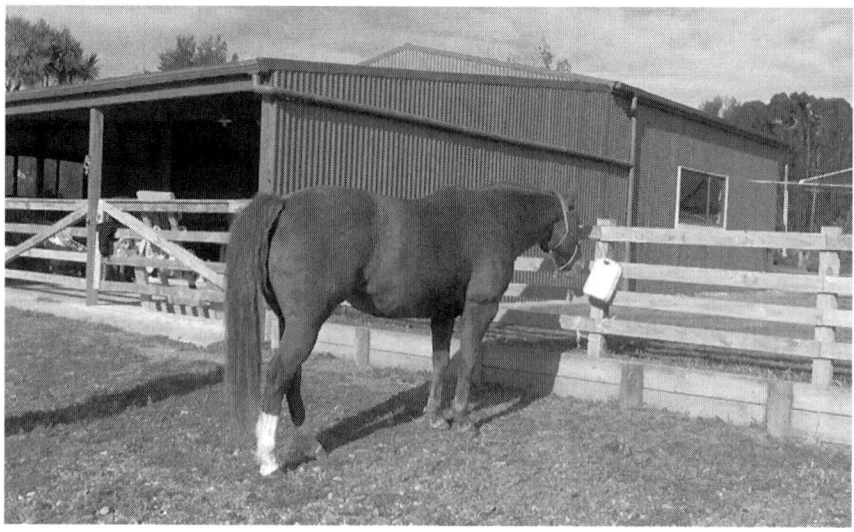

Boots has a long history of positive reinforcement for staying parked at a stationary nose target. We need the horse to be comfortable with nose targets if we want to use them as part of 'okay to repeat' signals.

PREREQUISITES:
- Horse and handler are clicker savvy.
- Horse is not hungry.
- Horse has a strong history of positive reinforcement for touching a target (see Chapter One).
- Handler is aware of moving in and out of his/her 'zero intent' posture (see Chapter Three).

ENVIRONMENT & MATERIALS:
- A work area where the horse is relaxed and confident.
- Ideally, the horse can see his buddies, but they can't interfere.
- A familiar target tied or set at the height of the horse's nose.
- Start with halter and lead on, with the lead draped over the horse's neck or back so it is easy to reach if the horse choses to walk away. If he moves away, quietly walk a circuit that brings you both back to the target; click&treat if the horse touches his nose to the target, then finish the session.
- If he chooses not to touch the target when you return to it, go back to a few sessions with a high rate of reinforcement for touching a series of targets hung around your training area, before returning to the task in this chapter.
- You can also have the horse at liberty and if he chooses to walk away, the session is automatically finished.
- Keep each session very short. Ideally always stop before the horse shows any desire to walk away, even if it means you only do one repeat. Mini-sessions where the horse is continually successful at earning his click&treat make for rapid learning and a willingness to 'do it again' next time.

- You are also showing the horse that it is okay to say, "I don't feel like doing that right now," without any value judgement on his behavior. You are giving him the choice about whether he wants to keep on working for clicks&treats, or he'd rather go away and do his own thing.

AIMS:

A. Horse realizes that the handler will stay at 'zero intent' unless he touches his nose to the target.

B. Handler waits patiently for the horse to touch the target as a sign that the horse is 'okay to repeat' the task.

C. Horse realizes that he can move away if he doesn't feel like playing.

D. Handler realizes that there are times when it is okay to let the horse have a 'say' in what will happen next.

VIDEO CLIP:

#156 HorseGym with Boots: OKAY TO REPEAT SIGNALS.

SLICES:

1. Horse touches nose to target: click&treat.

2. Handler allows horse to investigate any gear he is about to use (brush, spray bottle, clippers, halter, cover, saddle blanket, paste worming tube, saddle or harness, bridle): click&treat, maybe several times, depending on how comfortable the horse is with the item already.

3. If the horse is wary about the object, walk away backwards (or have another person walk away backwards holding it while you follow with the horse at the horse's pace) and have the horse follow; click&treat any sign of willingness to approach the

object more closely until he is able to put his nose on it to earn a click&treat.

4. Horses tend to follow things moving away from them and move away from things coming toward them. Yet most horse handlers expect a horse to stand still while they approach with an unusual object.

5. If we allow the horse the time to make up his own mind that an object is harmless, he will accept it as so. Horses naturally use approach and retreat whenever they come across something new. Life is much easier if we use their world view to facilitate our training, rather than restrict their movement and force them to accept something.

As a youngster, Boots found the bike scary. We walked along behind the bike moving away from us. We started out much further back than the left photo shows. In her own time (a matter of a few minutes) curiosity gradually replaced fear until she wanted to investigate the bike with her nose when it stopped moving away. I was careful to always keep a soft drape in the rope as we followed the bike together.

6. Handler lifts arm with brush (or whatever) toward the horse keeping it at a distance that maintains the horse's relative relaxation (under threshold*): click&treat.

7. Horse either leaves after the treat or touches the nose target again.
8. If the horse touches the target again, the handler repeats approaching the horse with the brush, careful to click&treat while the horse is still under threshold*, i.e. he still looks confident about what is going on.
9. After each click&treat, the handler resumes the 'zero intent*' position and waits for the horse to either touch the nose target again or take the option to leave.

Ideally the handler will stop each mini-session before the horse feels the need to walk away. If the horse leaves, it is also the end of that mini-session. The handler now has useful feedback*. He or she asked for more than the horse could offer comfortably at that time.

Done quietly and carefully with many mini-sessions that don't push the horse beyond his comfort zone*, the horse can usually relax into the new game which consists of the new things he has to allow if he wants to elicit more treats from the environment (his handler).

The horse's comfort zone will gradually expand to include the new task we are doing with him. At that point, the acquisition* stage is over, and we start to focus on fluidity*, generalization* and maintenance*, as outlined in Chapter 1.

Working for a food reward (even a tiny one like a strip of carrot) activates one of the most powerful seeking systems in the deepest part of the mammal brain.

Boots was out grazing when I set up this target and began organizing my camera. She has such a strong history of positive reinforcement with nose targets that she left her grass to come to the target and wait for me to be ready to film (i.e. play click&treat games with her).

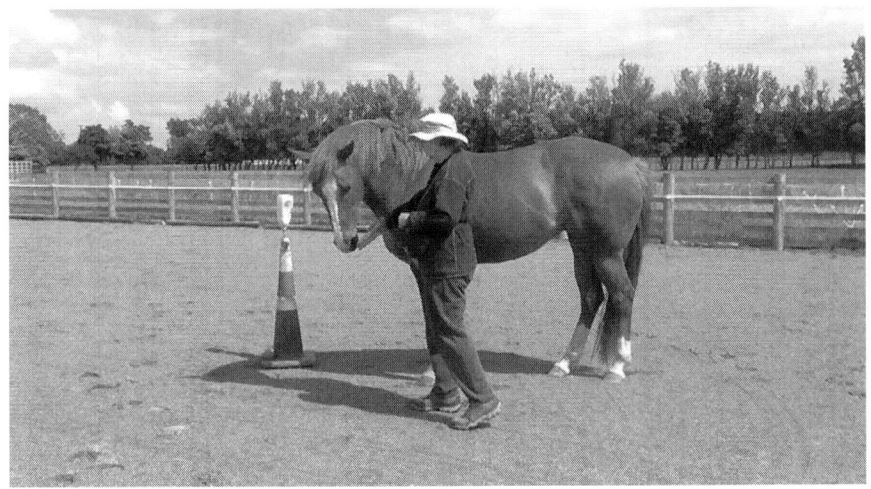

Boots has never loved brushing and stroking as some horses do, so it is nice to ask her permission for grooming. Here she is sniffing the brush (slice 2), which lets her know what I am hoping to do with her.

When Boots touches the target, I begin grooming. I start with one stroke on her neck before a click&treat. If she continues to touch the target after each click&treat, I gradually brush for longer and in more areas before each click&treat.

After each click&treat, I take up my 'zero intent' position and wait to see if she is going to touch the target again or walk away. Sometimes it takes her few seconds to enjoy her treat and have a think.

Here we have switched the brush for a Swedish Massage Roller, which is two round rotating wooden balls. Since it is a new object, I roll it on her neck once or twice before the first click&treat.

This is a video clip from a while ago which demonstrates the same idea. #4 HorseGym with Boots: Parking at a Nose Target.

'Okay to Proceed' with Mat Foot Targets

Another way to ensure consent or 'permission to proceed' is to ask the horse to park his feet on a mat. The horse's willingness to stay parked lets us know that he is okay for us to proceed.

'Okay to Proceed' is a little different from 'Okay to Repeat'. I use it for foot care which is a series of tasks rather than a repetition of the same task. Changing bandages and dealing with riding boots on and off, blankets on and off are also more in the line of 'procedures'.

A procedure like putting on riding or driving tack could also be thought of in the same way, although I found a nose target also worked well for tacking up.

Once we have taught standing on a mat with some duration, we can use the horse's willingness to stay there as a sign that he is probably okay for us to proceed with whatever we are doing. (See Chapter Two.)

VIDEO CLIP:

#157 HorseGym with Boots: 'OKAY TO PROCEED' WITH A MAT.

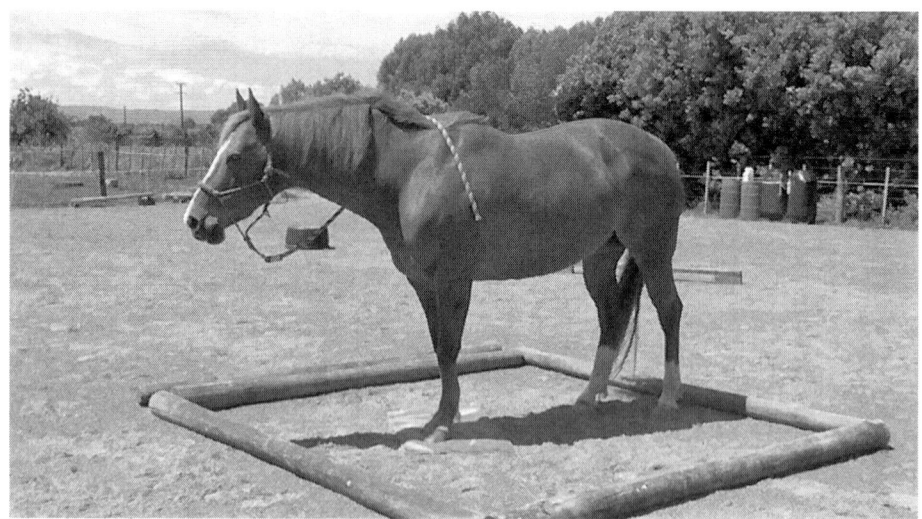

Boots has a long history of positive reinforcement for staying parked on a mat in a variety of different situations.

If we use a mat with frequent short sessions for teaching vet procedures or foot care, the horse will soon realize that the mat coming out means clicks&treats are on the way.

If the horse feels the need to move off the mat it is critical that we don't restrict or punish him in any way. We quietly walk a circuit together to return to the mat and halt on it:

click&treat for the halt on the mat. We must ensure that the mat always remains a desirable place in the horse's mind.

After returning to the mat, we can return to earlier slices with the task we are working on to find where the horse can still be continually successful, then end on a good note. Or we can use the mat to do something easy that the horse already knows to re-establish the mat as a good place to be.

Ideally, the handler will be able to read the horse's increasing body tension before the horse moves off the mat and take one of the two options above or initiate a relaxation break before resuming the training.

Even though something has obviously caught her attention, she is able to stay parked on the mat because of its long history of positive reinforcement.

Just as horses are conscious of any tension we hold in our bodies, so they are conscious when we let go of the tension.

Boots knows from many past sessions that our big mat means foot care. She willingly offers her first foot, for which I give her a click&treat. I then clean all her feet with another click&treat after I've cleaned <u>all</u> her feet.

Once the horse parks on a mat in a relaxed manner with duration, we can use his willingness to stay on the mat as a sign that he is okay to proceed with what we are doing. There is no penalty if the horse walks away. If he walks away, we have valuable feedback* about his state of emotional, mental and/or physical comfort at that point in time. In the photo Boots is about to get a treat for keeping her foot up.

Horse Specific 'Okay' Body Language Signals

To explore this concept with your horse, choose a simple task that the horse will probably find pleasant. Once the horse buys into the concept of giving us an 'okay to repeat' signal, we can expand to other physical care and vet procedures.

If you can choose one that is new to the horse it may be easier because it won't have the baggage of past experiences. But we can also add this new dimension to a task the horse already knows.

Once I became more consciously aware of these signals, I realized that Boots had been using them in a variety of contexts and I had been taking note of them. Once I began observing more closely, I soon realized that she had several signals for letting me know when it was 'okay to repeat'.

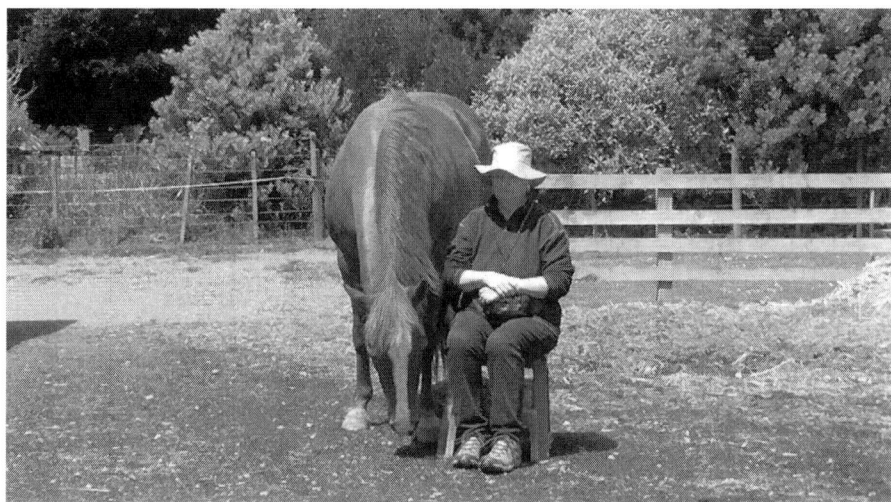

This is Boots' 'Okay to Rub Inside my Ear Again' signal. We played with this initially to explore 'okay to repeat' signals because it was not something I'd purposefully done with her before. I stay in 'zero intent' mode until she gives me this signal.

VIDEO CLIPS:

#154 HorseGym with Boots OKAY to REPEAT shows Boots' signal for rubbing the inside of her ear, which we had never done purposefully before. It also has an interlude of belly-scratching with a new tool.

#155 HorseGym with Boots OKAY to REPEAT for TOOTH INSPECTION: shows Boots' signals for allowing me to lift her lips to inspect her teeth.

Some other possibilities are:

- Targeting the eye to a cloth.
- Targeting the mouth to a paste worming tube.
- Simulating injections.
- Comfort with spray bottles.
- Comfort with scissors or clippers.
- Teaching specific tasks within a chained procedure such as comfort with saddle pad put on and removed, saddle put on and removed, girth tightened and loosened, handler putting foot in stirrup, handler leaning across horse, and so on.

PREREQUISITES:

- Horse and handler are clicker savvy*.

ENVIRONMENT & MATERIALS:

- A work area where the horse is relaxed and confident.
- The horse is not hungry.
- Ideally, the horse can see his buddies, but they can't interfere.
- Horse at liberty in a safe area. The horse needs to be free to move away if he no longer wants to take part.

AIMS:
- A. Handler is consistent with returning to 'zero intent' to wait for the horse to give his 'okay to repeat' signal.
- B. Horse learns that nothing will happen until he initiates it with his 'okay to repeat' signal.

SLICES:

The procedure is basically the same with any task.

1. Gently indicate to the horse what you would like to do; click&treat. Maybe repeat a couple of times to establish the task.
2. Then remove all signal pressure and take up your 'zero intent' position.
3. Observe the horse closely but don't stare at him with intent. Keep your body language totally relaxed. It may take a while for the horse to make a movement that seems significant.

    We have to be mindful that some horses have never been given a say in what is going to happen once they are haltered or confined in a small space, so it could take a long time for them to try something brand new to their experience.

    If you have played with your horse at liberty in the past, and allowed expression of opinion, it may all happen quickly.

4. When the horse makes a movement that you think is an expression of his willingness for you to repeat the task, quietly activate the task with short duration, then click&treat. When I did this with ear-rubbing, I initially rubbed only once or twice before the click&treat. Eventually I began rubbing a bit longer before the click&treat.
5. After the treat is delivered, return to 'zero intent' mode and wait for the horse to repeat his signal (he may

have, or develop, a variety of these signals, as Boots shows in the video clips).

6. As with most training, doing a little bit (three minutes or 20 treats) often is the key to rapid progress. It gives the horse time to process what has happened and often he is keen to repeat next time you set up the situation.

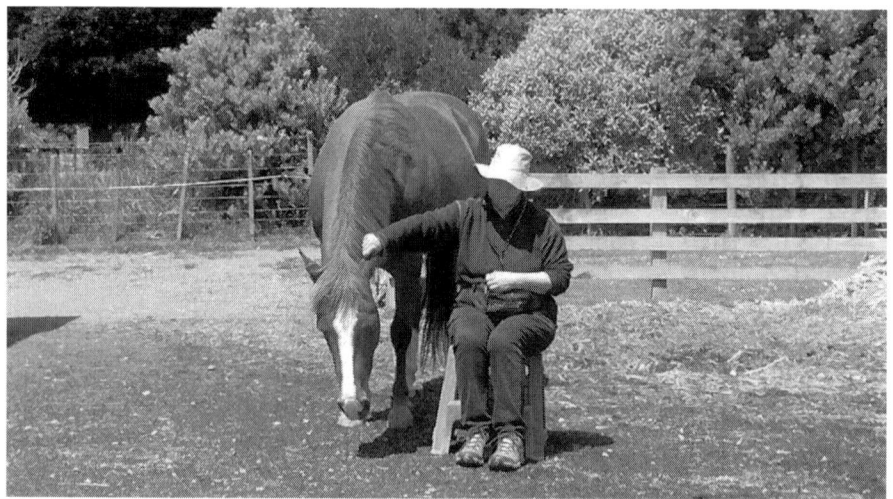

When she is okay for me to repeat rubbing inside her ear, Boots signals me by lowering her head beside me. After rubbing for a while, I click&treat.

It could be that ear-rubbing is intrinsically pleasant for a horse already relaxed in human company. Even if it is, I want the horse to eventually relate offering of an 'okay to repeat' signal to any task that will earn a click&treat.

Tasks like eye care and checking teeth and allowing skin pinching and toothpick pricking to prepare for inoculations will not be intrinsically pleasant.

All horses are different, both innately and due to their life experiences. Therefore, each horse and handler will together create a unique 'okay to repeat' signal language that works for them.

This is our tummy scratching task. Boots is not a horse that loves grooming, so it was a good task for us to seek out 'okay to repeat' signals.

One of Boots' several 'okay to repeat' signals is her 'smile' which she has used for a long time. She quickly added it to this context.

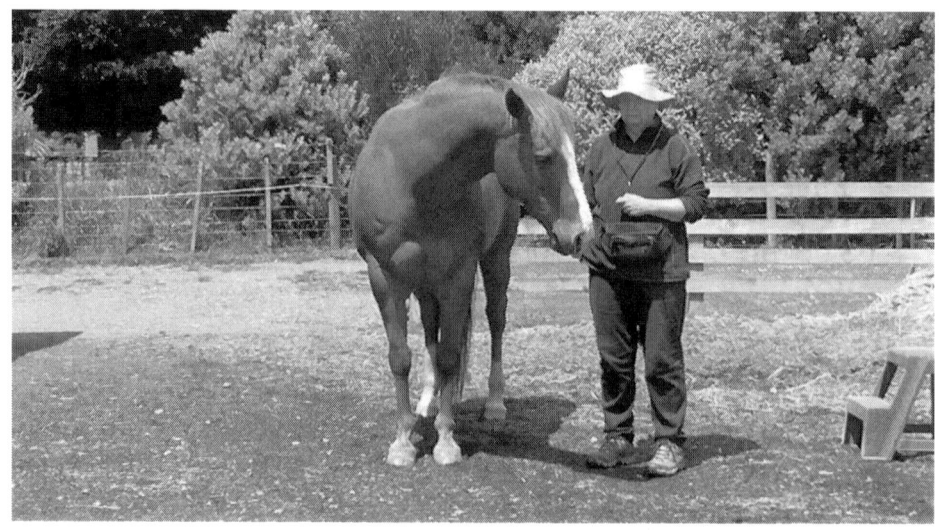

For the tummy-scratching task, she changed from dropping her head down as she did for ear-rubbing, to a momentary turn toward me followed by straightening her head again. It was distinctly different from 'mugging* the treat pouch' behavior.

The video clips do a much better job of demonstrating the flow of the training. So far, Boots' body language 'okay to repeat' signals include dropping her head, momentarily turning her head toward me, her smile, and offering to place her nose between my hands for tooth inspection.

If there is no consistency in our body language, horses tend to regard all of it as meaningless and tune it out.

Chapter Five

Targeting Body Parts to the Hand

INTRODUCTION:

Asking the horse to target various body parts to our hand requires precision with body language and signals. #130 *HorseGym with Boots* illustrates.

The clip mentioned above shows the body-part targeting tasks after about two years of working with them a little bit most days. This chapter looks at how to <u>begin</u> this most interesting process. Building precision was only possible after I trained myself to be crystal clear and consistent about the gesture signal I used for each body part.

 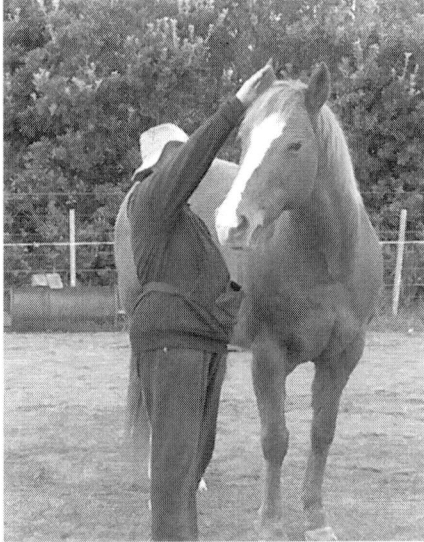

In the first photo, Boots is starting to bring her ear to my stationary hand. A second later she has pushed her ear against my hand.

The task I like to start with is targeting the chin to the palm of the hand. Beginning with a simple task allows you to build an awareness of the importance of:

- Your own body language.
- Signal clarity.
- Orientation to the horse.

You can then teach the targeting of other body parts when you are ready.

I suggest leaving the 'hip to hand' as the very last one you teach, and be sure to first have clear, consistent communication for asking the horse to move his hip away.

Some things we teach a horse can become problematic if people who have less horse savvy, and no knowledge of your signals, spend time with your horse. Some of the horse's movements can be mis-read, making things unsafe for both the other people and the horse.

Targeting body parts is fun to do when we are short on time or it's too hot, wet, cold, or muddy to be out and about.

I've started with targeting chin to hand, because it is probably the easiest one to establish the IDEA of targeting different body parts to our hand. It gives us a simple task to practice the following:

- Good timing of the click.
- Changing our body language from 'zero intent'* to 'intent'.
- Clarity of our signal asking for a particular body part.
- Consistent treat-delivery that keeps or returns the horse's head facing forward.

Building precision was only possible after I trained myself to be crystal clear and consistent about the gesture signal I used for each body part.

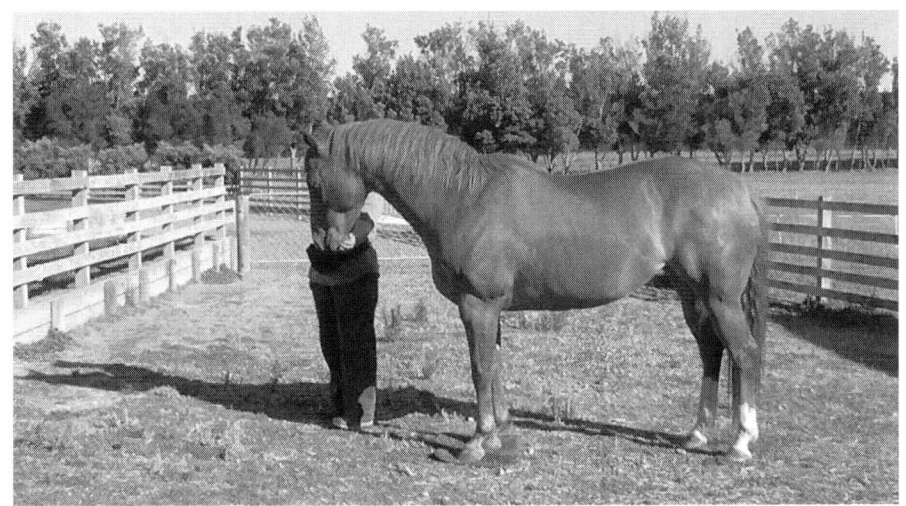

After targeting is well established, the first slice of teaching the horse to target chin-to-hand is to touch the chin with our palm; click&treat at the moment of touch and remove our hand.

PREREQUISITES:
1. Horse confidently touches his nose to a variety of different targets held in a variety of positions. In other words, he seeks out the target.
2. Horse confidently touches his nose to our outstretched fist in a variety of positions and with us standing beside him or in front of him.
3. Handler has developed a clear 'zero intent'* body language stance.
4. Horse understands the handler's 'zero intent' position, by remaining calmly facing forward for several seconds, rather than turning toward the treat pouch or pocket when the handler stands beside the horse's neck.
5. Handler is aware of a particular horse's 'Okay to Repeat' signals (see Chapter Four).

As a prerequisite, ensure the horse is comfortable with targeting your outstretched fist in a variety of positions.

ENVIRONMENT:

- Ideally, group mates in view but not able to interfere.
- Horse is not hungry, so he can focus on what we are teaching, rather than the treats.
- If the horse is mat-savvy, park his front feet on a mat when you begin teaching this.
- Ideally the horse is at liberty in a safe, enclosed area he finds comfortable. If necessary, you can teach this with halter and lead on.

VIDEO CLIP:

January 2018 Obstacle Challenges: Begin Body Targeting illustrates.

AIMS:

A. The horse willingly tucks his chin in to touch our hand held under his jaw.

B. The handler becomes more aware and fluid with slipping into and out of a 'zero intent' posture.

GENERAL COMMENTS:

1. Play with this in very short sessions. Stop when it feels good. Mini-sessions can fit in between other things that you are doing.

   Try for very short sessions (3-4 minutes) as frequently as possible. Every day is good, twice a day is even better, or several times amongst other things you are doing with the horse.

2. Stick with one body part until you and the horse are totally ho-hum with it. If the horse becomes confused, regaining confidence becomes our first aim. It is better to err on the side of making sure that targeting with a particular body-part is soundly in the horse's long-term memory, before moving to a new one.

3. When you are ready to introduce a second body part, the PROCESS is the same as the one outlined below for the chin.

4. To introduce another body part, begin each session with the one(s) you have already taught, then suggest the new spot by touching it, and progress through the thin-sliced process.

SLICES:

1. Touch the flat palm of your hand lightly to horse's chin; click&treat and immediately remove your hand.

2. Repeat several times so the horse can make the connection between the 'touch' and the click&treat.

3. Hold your open palm a tiny distance from the chin and wait for the horse to close the distance so he touches your hand: click&treat the instant you feel the touch. Also celebrate hugely (happy praise and a triple treat or jackpot).

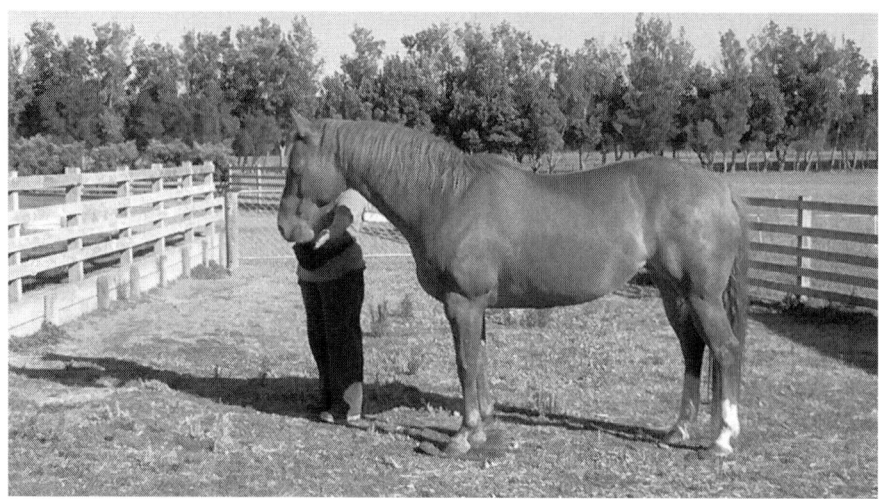

Slice 3: hold your hand a tiny distance from the horse's chin and wait for him to make the connection; click&treat the instant he does.

4. If you try 3 above, and the horse does not make the connection, resume with slice 2.

5. Once the horse is making the connection over a tiny distance, gradually increase the distance one millimetre at a time.

6. Early on in your teaching program, start each new session with a touch to the chin, to remind the horse about which task you are doing.

7. Once the horse clearly understands the task, lengthen the 'zero intent' position between repeats, to build a bit of 'dwell time'* between your requests. Build up the 'dwell time' in one-second increments.

8. Some horses will develop a little signal to tell you when they have finished chewing and are 'okay to repeat'* (see Chapter Four). Watch out for these and value them by doing a repeat. Boots illustrates this in the video clip.

9. Teach the targeting on either side of the horse. Some horses find it relatively easy to generalize something leaned on one side to the other side. Other horses find this more difficult. At any rate, always start again with Slice 1 on the opposite side.

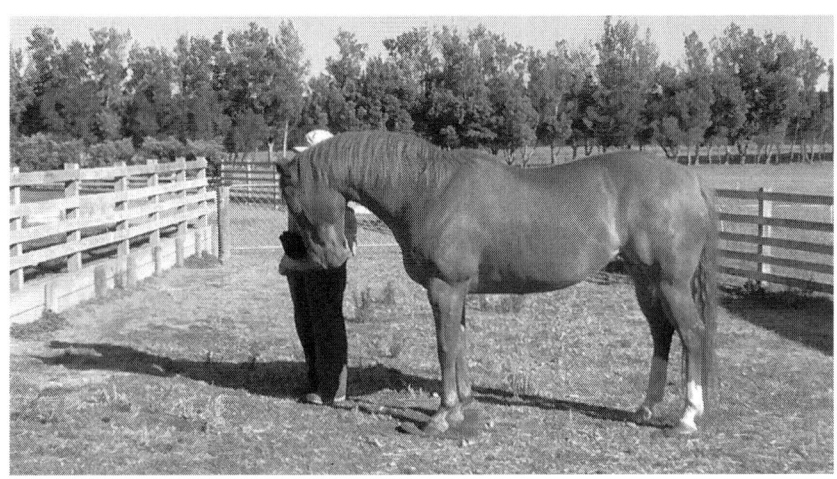

In this photo you can see that Boots is making a real effort to bring her chin back to touch my hand.

As the handler gets better and better at thin-slicing a large task into its smallest teachable parts, it becomes easier and easier for the horse to learn by being continually successful. It's this aspect of learning that makes a horse look forward to his sessions.

Eventually we can hold our hand well back and the horse will flex at the poll to make the connection.

GENERALIZATIONS:

Most of these generalizations are illustrated in the clip mentioned at the beginning of the chapter.

- Target ear to hand.
- Target eye to hand.
- Target forehead to hand
- Target top of nose to hand.
- Target knee to hand.
- Target shoulder to hand.
- Target hip to hand.
- Target hocks to hand.
- Target withers to hand.

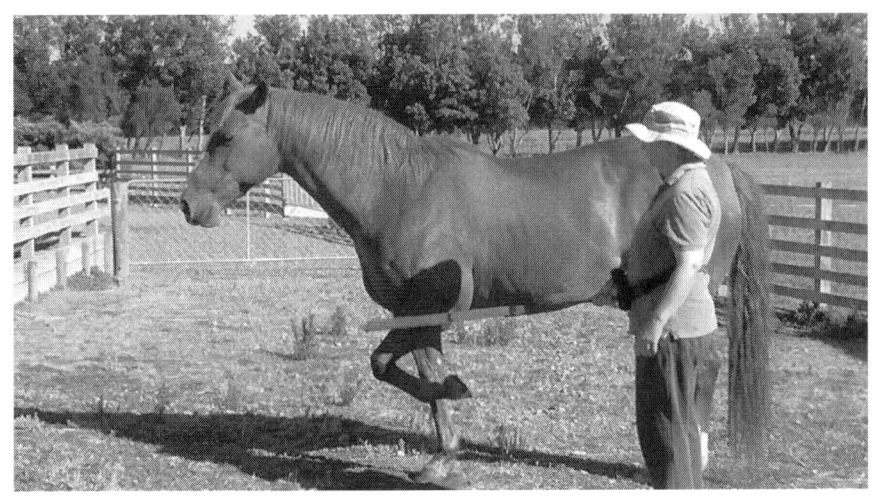

We can use the same procedure to teach the horse to target an object with his knee: first we click&treat when we touch the object to the knee. Then we hold it out a bit and wait for the horse to make the connection. This target is a light plastic tomato stake with bubble wrap taped around it.

Eventually we can substitute our hand for the target.

Use the same procedure for teaching the hip to target our hand. I recommend teaching this after all the others and only if you have first taught a clear signal for the horse to move his butt away from you. If other people handle your horse, this movement can be scary, unexpected and cause problems for the other handler and therefore for the horse.

Playing with body-part targeting is a unique way to get your horse to do various stretching exercises. They fit in nicely when it is too cold, hot or wet to do much else. They are also a nice way to begin time with the horse or as a set of 'end of session' exercises.

If we miss the horse's first attempt to solve a puzzle, he can think his idea was wrong, and it can be a while before he tries his first idea again.

Chapter Six

20 Steps Exercise

INTRODUCTION:

This is one of my favorite exercises. It is fun to do as a warm-up, a cool-down or if horse-time is short. If you are energetic you can eventually do it trotting.

This exercise encourages the horse to walk with us beside his neck or shoulder. It is a way of teaching 'leading' without the need to put pressure on the lead rope or use a lead rope at all.

The more precise we can be with our body language, the easier it is for the horse to read our intent*.

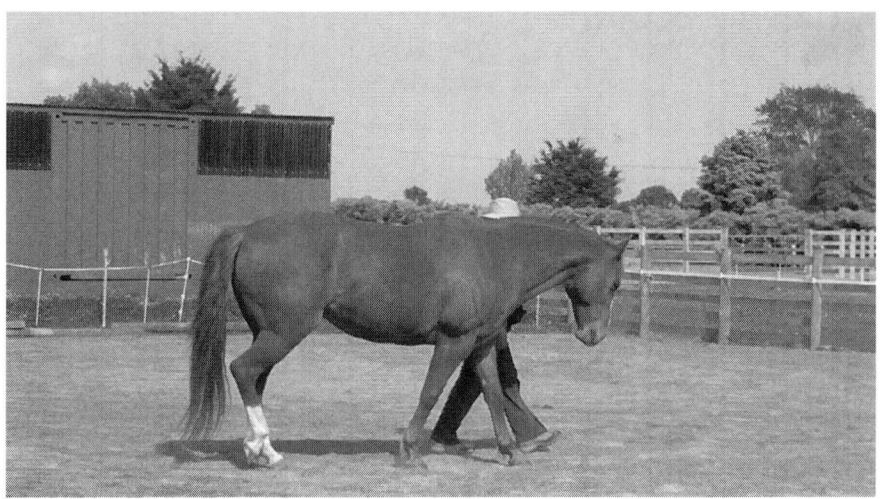

When we invite the horse to walk with us in the '20 Steps Exercise' we adjust our pace to the horse's natural pace, so we can walk 'in step' with each other.

When we do this task at liberty, it's easy for the horse to let us know if he is not in the mood to do things with us because he can peel off in his own direction.

If you have a safe, enclosed area, and protected contact is no longer needed, starting at liberty is ideal.

If the horse is exuberant and protected contact remains a good idea, you can still do this exercise with the horse at liberty by using a reverse round pen (person in the pen, horse moves around the outside of it) or a stretch of paddock fence. If your fencing is electric tape, make sure it is turned off.

Doing a little at a time keeps this exercise fresh and lively in the repertoire.

If protected contact is a good idea, we can set up a reverse round pen with uprights and fencing tape. The horse moves around the outside of the 'pen' while the handler stays inside. We can set up a size that best suits our present task.

The more precise we can be with our body language, the easier it is for the horse to read our intent.

A reverse round pen made with rails.

PREREQUISITES:
- Handler is aware of using breathing and body energy level to indicate 'energy up' before moving off and 'energy down' before coming to a halt.

Optional: The following prerequisites are nice but not essential. This task is a way of achieving or improving the three skills below.
- Horse walks smoothly beside the handler's shoulder.
- Horse understands 'Whoa' voice and body language signals.
- Horse willingly responds to 'Walk On' body language signals.

ENVIRONMENT & MATERIALS:
- A work area where the horse is relaxed and confident.
- Ideally, the horse can see his buddies, but they can't interfere.
- Horse is not hungry.
- A safe, enclosed area for working at liberty.

- If protected contact is the best choice, use a reverse round pen or use a paddock fence, whichever suits your situation best.
- If there are no other options, use halter and lead, keeping a non-influencing drape in the lead rope. A light-weight lead may be preferable.

AIMS:
  A. Handler refines clear 'walk-on' and 'halt' body language, energy levels and voice signals.
  B. Horse willingly mirrors the handler's energy changes and stays in position with his neck or shoulders beside the handler.

VIDEO CLIPS:

December 2017 Obstacle Challenge: 20 Steps Exercise illustrates.

#30 HorseGym with Boots illustrates Boots helping Zoë learn the process with halter and lead.

SLICES:
  1. Standing beside the horse's neck/shoulder, do the following pretty much all at the same time:
     - Raise torso and look ahead.
     - Breathe in deeply.
     - Gesture forward with the hand furthest from the horse.
     - Step off with your outside leg to walk one step using 'draw energy' to encourage the horse to walk with you. The horse can more easily see movement of your outside leg.

- Halt after one step by breathing out and releasing your energy; click&treat when your feet are stopped, even if the horse has moved out of position.
2. We will click&treat for EACH halt.
3. If the horse is a bit surprised and moves out of position, move YOURSELF back into position beside his neck/shoulder and start again, raising torso breathing in, gesturing and stepping off to walk on; slowing, breathing out and collapsing torso to stop. If you are consistent, the horse will begin to take note of your breathing and posture.

If you are on the other side of a barrier or fence from the horse, walk on and click&treat any indication that the horse is willing to come join you, then start again with 1 above.

4. It's ideal to start with the horse between the handler and a safe fence, so the option of swinging the hindquarters away is removed. I didn't show this part in the video clip.

If protected contact is necessary and the horse is unsure about what you want to do if you try using a reverse round pen or paddock fence, setting up a lane can work well because it reduces the horse's options. The horse walks in the lane and the handler walks on the outside of the lane.

Lanes can be set up with fencing tape and uprights next to a fence or made with bits and pieces like the one in the photo below.

Counter conditioning means putting a positive spin on something that is not part of normal wild horse life.

We can often make learning easier for the horse by organizing our training environment so that what we will click&treat is easy for the horse to discover, such as using a lane to initiate relaxed walking side-by-side together.

5. When one or two steps together is smooth, take three steps before the halt, click&treat.
6. When three steps together are smooth, take four steps before the halt, click&treat, and so on.
7. Each time you walk on, begin counting at 'one' again.
8. Stay with four-five steps until moving off together is smooth and the horse stays in position beside you for the halt.
9. Adjust how many steps you add before each halt and click&treat. It will depend on how fast the horse catches on to the pattern as well as how he is feeling that day.
10. With some horses you can soon add steps in 2's, 3's or 5's to reach the twenty steps.
11. If the horse gets lost or seems to forget, go back to where he can be successful and work with a smaller number of steps until you gain true confidence.
12. Gradually work up to 10, 15, then 20 steps before each halt, click&treat.

13. Asking for 20 steps before the click&treat, carried out on both sides of the horse, is usually plenty at one time.

Be sure to teach this walking on either side of the horse. One side may be easier. Start again from the beginning (along a fence or in a lane) for the second side. Some horses easily transfer new learning to the other side. Other horses find everything harder on one side.

Handlers usually must focus consciously on producing clear, consistent body language with the less dominant side of their body. If the horse's and handler's stiffer sides coincide, everything will feel a bit harder at first.

When a task feels equally smooth on either side of the horse, a big milestone has been achieved.

GENERALIZATIONS:
- If you started with a lane, move from the lane to working alongside a fence.
- Play the game in an open area, away from a fence-line.
- Teach, then add drawing the horse into arcs and turns with the horse on the outside of the turn (see photos coming up).
- Teach, then add walking arcs and turns toward the horse (counter-turns – see photos coming up).

Once I became consciously aware of 'okay' signals, I realized that Boots had been using them in a variety of contexts and I had been taking note of them

Our body language for asking the horse to turn when we are on the inside of the turn is to clearly swivel our body axis <u>away</u> from the horse to 'draw' him around with us.

Here I'm encouraging Boots to turn with me by walking together around a marker toward a mat where she will halt for a click&treat. Having the mat destination gives her a reason to move around the corner with precision. For a turn where the handler is on the inside, the handler has to slow down, but remain active enough to model the energy level the horse needs to negotiate the turn. As mentioned already, body language for this turn is to turn the body axis away from the horse and lean away a bit to 'draw' the horse around the curve. I also add a voice signal.

Each time we walk around one of these two markers, we head for the mat in the center for a halt: click&treat.

Here we are practicing our counter-turn which is when the handler is on the outside of the turn. The key is to swivel the axis of our body toward the horse. For teaching I also gesture with my outside hand and use a voice signal. For this turn, the handler must stride out to stay in position beside the horse, but not with so much energy that the horse speeds, losing synchronization and connection.

We have completed the counter-turn in the previous two photos and returned to the mat for a click&treat. Setting up two markers like this with a mat in the middle allows us to walk in a figure 8 pattern so we can practice turns where the handler is on the inside as well as counter-turns where the handler is on the outside of the turn.

- Teach, then add a few steps of back-up every now and then.
- If fitness allows, play at jog or trot.

Handlers must use conscious focus to producing clear, consistent body language with the less dominant side of their body.

If the horse's and handler's stiffer sides coincide, everything will feel a bit harder on that side until practice strengthens their muscle memories.

Chapter Seven

Soft Response to Rope Signals

INTRODUCTION:

It's not uncommon for a horse to have bad feelings or mixed emotions about halters and ropes. My book *Walking with Horses*, has a detailed section about developing a horse's willingness to put his nose into a halter.

To help horses deal well with captivity, it is important to give careful attention to building their confidence with halters and lead ropes.

Essentially, we want a halter and rope on the horse to feel similar to when we put on our 'work clothes'. It becomes an outfit or uniform related to the work we do. If we work for an organization or with other people, we adjust our work behavior to what is appropriate for our job.

In the same way, a horse carefully educated about halters and ropes will recognize that he is wearing his 'uniform' and relate it to certain ways of behaving. Mainly, it limits his behavior choices. Ideally it also encourages him to pay careful attention to requests made via messages sent along the rope. The softer and more precise our rope handling, the better the deal for our horse.

It is astounding to see what some domestic horses are forced to put up with in, on and around their heads.

I've asked Boots to walk out around the barrel and come back toward me. I'm also using body language and voice signals, so the rope message can be extremely subtle. The weight of the rope itself gives a directional signal on her halter.

Horses' faces are incredibly sensitive, rich in nerves throughout the surface. Ears, eyes, nose and mouth (and all their related nerves) are all in close proximity. The whiskers above the eyes and around the muzzle (each with a direct link to the brain) are essential safety features for horses to feel the plants and terrain when they are grazing.

It would be weird for someone to come up and start fondling our face, yet people seem to believe it is perfectly all right to do this to a horse.

I was teaching the 'horseman's handshake' which is to hold out our fist and let the horse close the last inch of distance to make the contact, then walk away. Face fondling had no place at all in the presentation. Yet almost every one of the over twenty people there, when invited to walk up and 'greet' the horse, tried to <u>also</u> put their hand on the horse's face.

It is astounding to see what some domestic horses are forced to put up with in, on and around their heads. Bits on the sensitive membranes of their mouths, mouths tightly tied shut, chains around the nose, curb straps behind the chin, tight straps behind and in front of the ears, halter or bridle straps close to the eyes, rope halters with knots lying on the nerve pathway, halters put on so the nose band lies on the soft cartilage of the lower nose, blinkers on driving horses rubbing eyelashes.

Halters and lead ropes are necessary, but how we teach the horse about them, and how we use them, makes a big difference to the horse's quality of life.

We can use the lead rope to send text messages. But, obviously, we must first carefully teach the horse what the 'letters' of our text mean. The lighter the pressure of our 'texting', the lighter the horse's responses can be. In other words, the horse can only be as light in his responses to rope messages as we are light and consistent in the way we send them.

A rope is a way of 'holding hands' with our horse, not a tether kept tight to stop the horse escaping our influence. There is nothing so heartbreaking as seeing a gasping dog at the end of a tight leash or a horse struggling to understand why the tightness of the rope won't go away, no matter what he does.

The key to sensitive, precise rope handling is in keeping the rope slack except for the brief moments it is sending a message to the horse. The instant the horse complies with our request, the slack is returned to the rope. It is the instant release of rope pressure, plus the simultaneous click and accompanying treat, that enable the horse to understand what he must do to gain the release and the reward.

When we lead, long-rein or ride a horse, it does not take much movement of the head to cause the horse to change direction. The task in this chapter is not an extreme flexion exercise. It is an exercise to see how softly we can give what will become our 'please change direction' signals once the horse is moving.

Teaching a horse with no rope experience is usually easier than teaching a horse who has had rough treatment with ropes. In the second case, you must adjust your training plan to help overcome any anxiety the horse carries from previous handling. You may have to spend a great deal of time with click&treat for putting your hand on the rope, for picking up the rope, for putting the lightest feel on the rope, in order to overcome fear or anxiety reactions.

PREREQUISITES:

- Horse is comfortable wearing a halter.
- Horse is comfortable with a lead rope.
- Horse and handler are clicker savvy; horse knows all about touching targets to earn a click&treat.
- Horse understands standing on a mat with duration. (See Chapter Two).
- For the early sessions, it's helpful to have the horse standing with his butt in a safe corner so that backing up and swinging the hind end away are not options.

   The first slices will therefore involve making sure the horse is comfortable and relaxed standing with his hind end in a corner.

The first slice is to ensure that the horse is totally comfortable standing with his butt in a corner. Parking the front feet on a mat gives him a reason to stay there.

ENVIRONMENT & MATERIALS:
1. A work area where the horse is relaxed.
2. Ideally, the horse can see his buddies, but they can't interfere.
3. Horse is not hungry.
4. A safe corner the horse can stand in confidently. A safe corner is one where there is no chance of the horse putting a leg through wire or rails if he steps back or sideways.

   Hedges, sides of buildings or a corner made with barrels or jump stands and rails tend to be the safest. Even a raised rail or a log behind the horse plus a small barrier on the far side of the horse might be enough of a corner.
5. A familiar mat to park or 'station' the horse (see Chapter Two).
6. A familiar hand-held target. A small target, like a plastic water bottle or plastic disc, is easier than a target on a long stick (see Chapter One).
7. When using the halter touch signal via the rope, be ready to click&treat for even the tiniest turn of the head at first. If we miss the horse's first attempt to solve a puzzle, he can think his idea was wrong, and it can take a while for him to try it again.

AIMS:
   A. To have the horse comfortable standing with his butt in a safe corner.
   B. To teach an 'anchor task' that precedes our request to turn the head.
   C. Use a target to teach head flexion to right and left; no rope.
   D. Add 'right' and 'left' voice signals to the task.

E. Teach soft lateral flexion (turning the head right or left) using a gentle touch on the halter via a rope until it feels equally smooth to the right and the left.

F. Generalize the task to different places and situations.

VIDEO CLIPS:

September 2018 Challenge: Soft Rope Response Clip One.

September 2018 Challenge: Soft Rope Response Clip Two.

SLICES:

A: Standing Comfortably in a Corner

Introduce the horse to the corner in small, easy steps. Thin-slice the process to what your horse needs. Use a familiar mat to indicate where you would like his front feet to be (see Chapter Two). Three kinds of corners are shown in the video clips.

- If the horse knows about yielding hindquarters and forequarters, we can use these to adjust his position.
- Or we can lead him through the corner and back him into it (see Chapters Eight and Nine).
- If we are using a rail, half-barrel or log as a barrier behind the horse, we can walk him over it and halt with it behind him.
- Play with standing the hind end in as many safe corners as you can find or set up, to generalize the 'corner comfort task' to different situations.

B: Teach an Anchor Task*

In the same way that music is made up of notes and the pauses between the notes, we must have pauses between asking the horse to repeat the same task. Because the horse is at halt for this challenge, the anchor task* creates the pauses between our requests.

We begin teaching the anchor task once the horse is comfortable standing with his hind end in a corner, front feet on a mat, with reasonable duration (at least 3-4 seconds).

An anchor task is what we do to 'set the stage' for what we will do next. For example, when I play with targeting body parts to my hand with Boots, our anchor task is lifting a front knee to my hand. It tells her what game we are about to play. (See Chapter Five.)

As an anchor task for this behavior, I've chosen to rest my nearest hand lightly behind Boots' withers while she keeps her head forward. It is the position my hand would be if I were to lift the reins in preparation to giving a signal while riding. You might prefer a different anchor task. The key is that the horse calmly remains facing forward.

This is our 'anchor behavior' for this task: my arm resting lightly behind her withers while she keeps her head forward.

With Boots, this was a bit tricky because I use the same anchor position when we do belly crunches while I stand beside her. The handler's body orientation is often a large part of an anchor task.

I decided that Boots is far enough along in her training to learn to pause in this anchor position and wait for the next signal to find out whether a crunch or head flexion is the hot topic of the moment. You'll see in the video clips that we have a couple of conversations about this.

SLICES:
- Stand beside the horse's withers.
- Lightly rest your near hand on the withers.
- Click&treat when the horse's head is straight, or he is moving his head into the 'straight' position. When he turns his head toward you, ignore it and move your treat pouch furthest away from the horse. If you are relaxed and persistent, he will eventually realize that the click&treat are only forthcoming when he keeps his head straight.
- Step forward to deliver the treat so the horse keeps his head straight, then step back into position beside the withers.
- Repeat until the horse confidently stays facing forward for 3-4 seconds before you click&treat.

C: Lateral Flexion to a Target

Have a familiar target handy tucked behind you out of sight while you review the anchor task.

1. When the horse stands reliably with his head forward in the anchor position for 3-4 seconds, bring the target forward so he has to turn his head <u>a little bit</u> to touch it: click and step forward so he straightens his head to receive the treat. At the same time, put the target out of sight behind your back.

   It takes a bit of practice to get all this smooth. If you can, practice the mechanics with another person to put the process into your muscle memory.

2. Step back beside the withers and return your hand to his withers: click&treat for head forward until that is firmly established <u>again</u> (3-4 second duration).

   Be patient about establishing (and frequently re-establishing) this step because clever horses will want to skip straight from your anchor (hand on withers) to telling you that they know what to do – turn toward you (as Boots does in Clip Two).

3. Repeat 2 above until the horse reliably waits for you to produce the target before turning his head. If he turns without your signal, spend more click&treat time on facing forward.

4. Make sure you keep the target out of view behind your back when you are not in the act of presenting it to the horse. If bending toward the target is harder, spend more time on asking for the bend.

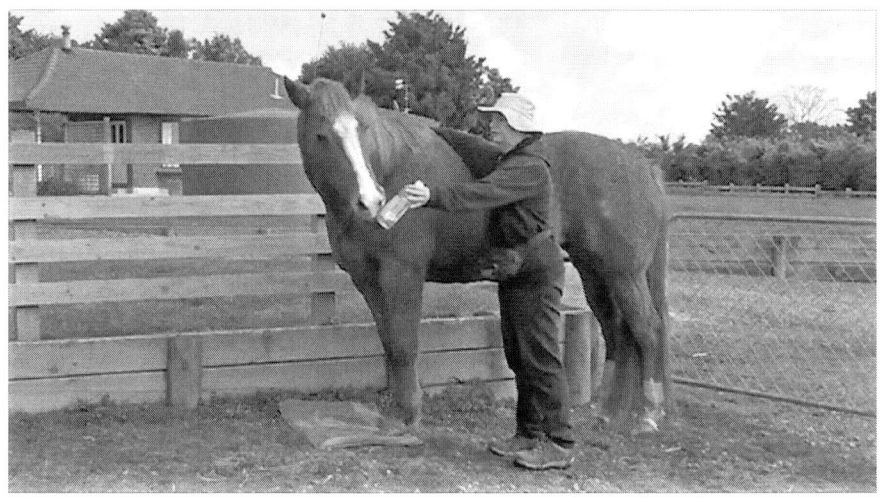

I present the target for Boots to bring her nose around to the left: click as her nose touches the target.

I put the target 'out of play' behind my back as I step forward to deliver the treat in a position which causes her to straighten her head again.

D. Add Voice Signals

- When slices 3 and 4 above feel reliable, add voice signals.

- You will obviously want different voice signals for right and left. Voice signals need to be short, clear, and sound different from other voice signals you use.

  I use "and Gee" for right. I use "and Left" for left. "Haw" for left sounds too much like "Whoa" which we use a lot. The "and" in front of the key word is a bit of a preparatory signal that lets the horse know a request is coming. My voice emphasis is on the key word.

- Some horses do better if you teach something thoroughly on one side, then repeat from the beginning on the other side.

- Some horses may cope well with doing a little bit on each side from the beginning.

- Some handlers do better when teaching the task thoroughly on one side first.

E. Adding the Rope

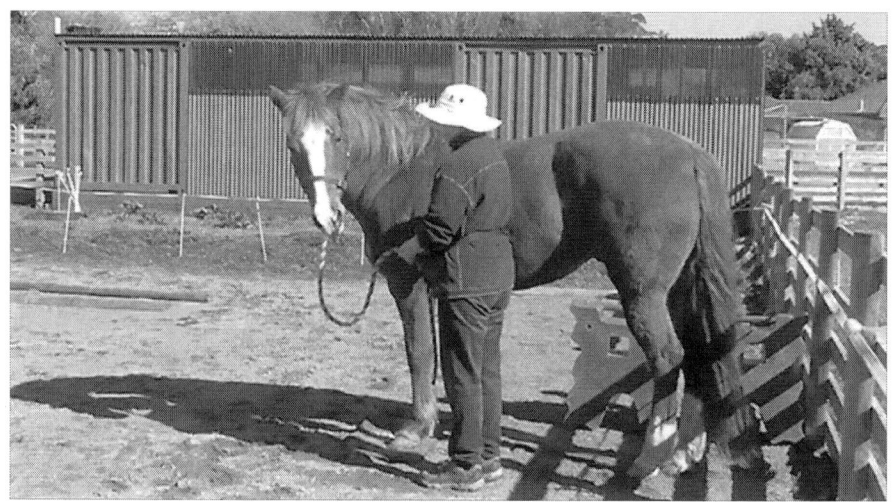

We are demonstrating a different corner. Very light 'milking of the rope' has caused Boots to turn her head toward me. I have clicked and am about to deliver the treat by stepping forward, so she straightens her head to retrieve the treat.

VIDEO CLIPS THREE AND FOUR:

September 2018 Challenge: Soft Rope Response Clip Three.

September 2018 Challenge: Soft Rope Response Clip Four.

SLICES:

1. Stand beside the horse's ribs just behind the withers, facing forward. Hold the rope in the hand closest to the horse. Keep a drape or 'smile' in the rope. Ensure that the horse can stay facing forward in a relaxed manner for 3-4 seconds <u>in the presence of the rope</u>; click&treat.

   His response when the rope is added to the task will give you valuable feedback about his feelings relating to ropes. This slice might take a while with a horse uncomfortable with ropes.

2. When 1 above is ho-hum, say your voice signal and quietly use both hands to gently 'milk' the rope so it puts light pressure on the halter, looking for the slightest 'give' of the horse's nose toward you. Release at the same time as you click. Step forward to deliver the treat in a way that has the horse straighten his head again.

3. Work with 1 and 2 above until the horse waits for the touch signal on the halter and willingly yields his nose. If he turns before you give the rope signal, spend more click&treat time on keeping the nose forward.

4. If he begins to turn his head as soon as you move back into position beside his withers, also go back to click&treat for a straight head.

5. Some horses catch on very quickly. Others may need many short sessions. Sessions of three-four minutes are usually best. They can be fitted in-between chores or other things you are doing with the horse.

6. Each time we return to start a new short session after doing other things, we bring a fresh 'new start' which is good to keep both the handler and the horse relaxed and looking forward to another session.

F: Generalizations (Illustrated in Video Clip Four.)

1. Once the whole task is smooth and ho-hum on both sides of the horse, move away from corners but still use a mat. Do the task with the mat in a variety of different places.

2. Once 1 above is good in lots of places, omit the mat and again work in a variety of places.

3. With the halter and lead still on, the gesture of 'milking the rope' can become a distinctive hand signal that can eventually be used to draw the horse right or left at liberty.

4. Once the horse understands the halter touch signal via the rope, plus the voice signal, the anchor task can morph into just standing quietly together with zero intent* (see Chapter Three).

5. Use the voice and touch signals (as well as your body language) while in motion to change direction, keeping the pressure on the rope as light as possible and emphasizing body language as outlined at the end of Chapter Six.

   We want to get in the habit of using the soft rope or rein signals learned at the halt whenever we are using a lead rope or rein to ask the horse to change direction while moving.

6. The YouTube playlist called *Developing Soft Rein Response* has a series of four clips that give further ideas about how we can generalize the task further using reins but without being mounted. This is the link to the first clip in the playlist.

7. Building a strong history of response to directional voice signals is most helpful if you are planning to teach long-reining and if you take part in Horse Agility.

This would not be safe without having a soft rope response in place, carefully taught at home in a variety of contexts.

Life is much easier if we use the horse's world view to facilitate our training, rather than restrict their movement and force them to accept something.

Notes:

Chapter Eight

The Finesse Back-Up

INTRODUCTION:

At one point a friend and I came up with 29 different ways of backing up a horse, including groundwork, long-reining and riding. This Finesse Back-Up is one of my favorites when I need to maneuver my horse on the ground.

I learned the essence of the process outlined in this chapter from Alex Kurland, a true pioneer of equine clicker training. Using corners to first teach this skill manages the environment so that stepping back makes sense to the horse right from the beginning.

This is a corner created with a fence and an open gate. Before teaching the back-up, we want the horse totally comfortable standing with his face in a corner.

PREREQUISITES:

- Horse will step forward to put his nose on a target and step back when the treat is delivered near his chest. (See photos below.) Chapter One looks in detail at introducing horses to targets.

- Horse is familiar with a 'back' voice signal given at the precise moment he steps back to retrieve the treat held near his chest.

- Handler easily slips into and out of 'zero intent*' so the horse clearly knows when he can relax in a 'wait' and when he is being asked to move. (See Chapter Three.)

- Horse willingly walks between the handler and a fence or similar barrier.

First, I ask Boots to reach across the fence to put her nose on the target. This is illustrated in the first of the video clips mentioned below.

Then I hold the treat toward her chest, so she moves back a step or two in order to retrieve the treat from my hand. I say, "Back" during the movement to begin establishing a clear voice 'back-up' signal I can later use in other situations.

ENVIRONMENT & MATERIALS:

- A work area where the horse is relaxed and confident.
- Ideally, the horse can see his buddies, but they can't interfere.
- Horse is not hungry.
- Target (on a long handle if possible), a low fence or barrier to work across.
- Halter and lead, although Part A is best done with the horse at liberty.
- A shorter 8 ft lead is easier to manage for this task.
- A safe corner made with a fence and barrier at 90 degrees to the fence, e.g. a fence and open gate, or two chest-high barriers set at a 90-degree angle.
- Mat (optional). A mat can make it easier for a mat-savvy horse to settle into standing in a corner.

AIMS:
- A. Teach or consolidate clear voice and body language intent* 'back' signals.
- B. Handler consistently uses precise body orientation, clear body language, and voice 'back' signals.
- C. Horse willingly steps backward from a halt on request, ideally in a straight line.
- D. Horse smoothly shifts from walking forward to stepping backwards on request.

CLIPS:

March 2018 Obstacle Challenge: Backing Up Part 1.

March 2018 Obstacle Challenge: Backing Up Part 2.

SLICES:

A. The 'Back' Body Language, Intent and Voice Signals.

1. Organize a relatively low barrier where the handler can be on one side and the horse on the other side (as in the two photos above.) It should be easy for the horse to stretch his head over the barrier to put his nose on a target, and for the handler to reach across the barrier to present the treat near the horse's chest.
2. Offer the target so the horse steps forward and reaches across the barrier to touch his nose to it. Click.
3. Put the target 'out of play' behind you while you take the treat out of your pocket or pouch, then step toward the horse and reach your arm across the barrier toward the horse's chest so the horse takes a step back to retrieve the treat from your hand. Say your voice 'back' signal while the horse is stepping back. Be aware of where your head is in relation to the horse's head.

4. If possible, set up this task in different places until it is fluid for both horse and handler. We want the horse to be tuned in to the "Back" voice signal as well as our intent. It will make it easier for him to understand the back-up request in other contexts.

B. Getting Comfortable in a Corner

1. Set up a safe corner with a gate or a barrier set at right angles to a fence.
2. Walk the horse into the corner and halt. The handler is on the open side of the corner. If the horse finds it hard to stand relaxed in the corner, and you have taught him to love standing his front feet on a mat, use a mat for your 'halt' position. Click&treat for the halt.

The first slice is to make sure that the horse can comfortably stand in a corner and wait for a few seconds. For the first lessons, I put a mat in the corner target (see Chapter 2).

3. Relax into zero intent* and ask the horse to 'wait' for a few seconds standing in the corner keeping his nose forward. Click&treat this 'wait' task until the horse is

relaxed standing in the corner keeping his head straight.

4. Walk the horse out of the corner, walk a loop and come back to park in the corner again. Click&treat the halt.

   This bit is not on the video clip but when first teaching this task, we want the horse totally comfortable standing in a corner. It's helpful to generalize to several different corners if you have them available or can set them up.

Once the horse readily parks calmly in the corner, we can begin to teach the Finesse Back-Up. I call it that because it requires gently running a hand or fingers up the rope toward the halter, until we reach a point of contact to which the horse responds.

Each horse will be different. I had trouble having Boots demonstrate this part clearly because she knows the task so well that she reads the very beginning of my orientation/body language sentence and steps back right away.

If we teach this well, the horse will step back as soon as we begin to turn with intent, even before we use our voice signal. Our hand on the rope eventually becomes redundant.

This is tricky to explain in words. Hopefully the video clips and pictures will make it clear.

Two terms explained:

<u>Outside hand</u> refers to the hand furthest away from the horse.

<u>Inside hand</u> refers to the hand nearest the horse.

These obviously change depending on which side of the horse you are on, and whether you are shoulder-to-shoulder with the horse both facing the same direction, or you are face to face with the horse.

C: The Finesse Back-Up Maneuver

1. Begin beside the horse's neck facing the same direction as the horse. You are going to smoothly pivot 180 degrees, so you face behind the horse, standing a little bit to one side of him.

*AS WELL: ***In the moment **before** you pivot...****

2. Gently reach <u>across</u> your body with your 'outside hand' and slide it quietly up the rope to a point of contact to which the horse responds.

At first, this may be right up to the snap on the halter (or if using a rope halter, even beyond the snap to hold the bottom of the halter) so you can give the horse a direct backwards *feel* on the halter.

As you pivot to face the horse, what *was* your 'outside hand' becomes your 'inside hand' — the one nearest the horse.

Notes:

Bridget (with a great look of concentration because this was her first time doing this) has reached across her body with her outside hand and is about to slide it gently up the rope toward the halter as she pivots to face behind Smoky. Once she has pivoted, this hand will become her inside hand because it will be closest to the horse.

3. Then simply keep a steady 'hold' tension on the rope as you bring up your energy and intent and use your 'back' voice signal. This change in your stance causes the horse slight discomfort by making him feel unbalanced.

We want him to work out that he can regain his balance/comfort by moving back. Because he's in a corner, his easiest choice is to step backward to regain his balance. Our first *click point** is the moment he thinks of moving back which you can notice because his weight starts to shift back.

4. When first teaching this task, release your 'hold' and simultaneously click&treat at the horse's <u>smallest inclination</u> to shift his weight back. After the treat, walk a circuit, return to the corner, and ask again.

5. Once the horse is readily shifting his weight back, release the rope pressure slightly as his weight shifts, then slide gently up the rope again and 'hold' a bit longer to get a full step back; click&treat. Drop your signaling hand off the rope as soon as you get backward movement. Walk a circuit, return to the corner, and ask again.

   If the horse has a good understanding of your 'back' voice signal and your intent body language, he may easily step back right away.

6. Keep each session short and stay with each slice until you are both ho-hum with it. Work with a safe barrier on the far side of the horse to help build the habit of straightness.

7. Teach all the slices on either side of the horse.

8. As he begins to understand, over multiple sessions, gradually ask for two steps, then three steps and so on, before the click&treat. The horse will soon know that relaxing your intent body language means he can stop backing; click&treat.

Bits of backing between doing other things is healthier for body and soul than doing a lot of it at one time. Stop a session if you feel any hint of frustration.

Trust that the horse is always doing the best he can at that moment.

I've pivoted to face behind Boots and my right hand is in position on the rope. Because Boots knows this well, I seldom need to do more than turn toward her and use the intent of my body language. She is already in the act of stepping backwards. As soon as the horse responds, I take the hand nearest the horse off the rope.

9. Still with a safe barrier on the far side of the horse, ask for two or three back-up sequences (of several steps each) in a row, with release, click&treat for each one. Then ask the horse to step forward into the corner again; click&treat.

10. Build a little dancing rhythm of movement: back up = click&treat. Forward into corner = click&treat. Back up = click&treat, and so on. After about three of these, do something else or relax for a while.

11. Gradually, over many short sessions, ask for more steps back until the horse willingly offers as many as you like.

Generalizations

1. Teach the whole process on the horse's other side.
2. Move away from the fence and use only a low <u>raised</u> rail on the far side.
3. Repeat with a ground rail along the far side of the horse.
4. Check to see how well the horse can do the Finesse Back-Up with no fence or rail on his far side.

   If you lose straightness at any point, return to using a fence or rail on the far side. If the horse begins to shift his hind end away from you, you can straighten his body by touching his neck to move it away from you, which will straighten out his body.

   Many horses find it hard to back in a straight line because they naturally push off harder with one hind leg. With frequent short backing sessions between two rails on the ground, or a narrow lane, the horse will learn to compensate for his unevenness.

5. Back through increasingly narrow spaces; e.g. two barrels, gates, into and out of stalls or pens, always being careful that the horse does not catch his hip on an upright.

Notes:

This was the result of a 30-day task-building training series. We spent 5-6 minutes on it each day. You can see that Boots has a natural tendency to veer to her right as she backs up. Her left hind foot pushes off more strongly than her right hind foot. She feels the barrel behind her in the first photo, and quickly corrects herself, as you can see in the second photo.

If you want to see each day's clip for the task described above, they are all in one playlist called, *Back Up to Mounting Block*.

Backing up while facing the same direction as the horse (as in most of the playlist) is the topic of Chapter Nine.

6. Back through lanes with sides.
7. Back along a track or trail.
8. Back down slopes and up slopes. Start with gentle inclines.
9. Back through corners.
10. Back around a square of rails – outside or inside the square.
11. Back an L-bend of rails.
12. Back a U-bend of rails.

13. Back a Z-bend of rails.
14. Back in a circle.

    When asking the horse to back up while you face him, moving his head a bit to his left (your right) will cause his butt to move to his right (your left).

    And vice versa if you move his head a little bit to his right, his butt will move to his left. If you want him to back straight, ask his head to stay straight.

15. Weave backwards (you need to have signals to direct his butt to the right, to the left and to keep it straight).
16. Back into a trailer or trailer simulation.

Bits of backing between doing other things is healthier for body and soul than doing a lot of it at one time. Stop a session if you feel any hint of frustration. The horse is always doing the best he can at that moment.

As you work through the generalizations thoughtfully, the precision of your body language will improve, and the precision of your horse's movements will follow.

Notes:

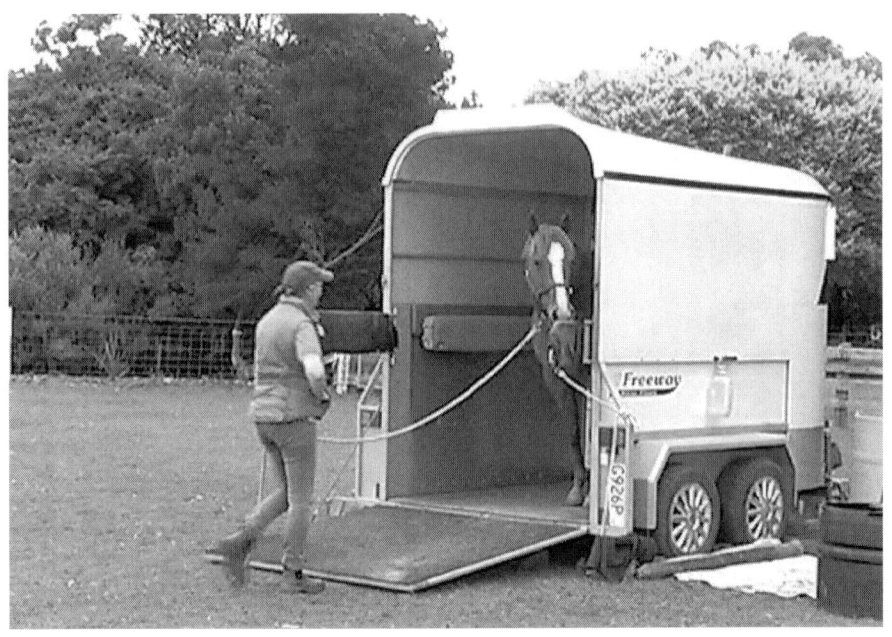

Teaching Boots to back up a slope was one of the slices I used to prepare her for backing up the ramp into the horse trailer, which we did just for fun. Some horses prefer to travel facing backwards.

In case you are wondering about using a trailer while not hitched to a vehicle, it was well-blocked front, back and both sides.

Eventually we can keep our feet still while asking the horse to back up. Then it is fun to generalize that skill to a variety of situations such as Boots' demonstration of backing through a set of pool noodles.

As you work through the generalizations thoughtfully, the precision of your body language will improve, and the precision of your horse's movements will follow.

Notes:

Chapter Nine

Backing Up Shoulder-to-Shoulder

INTRODUCTION:

This exercise is good for working on handler precision. It requires the handler to stay in position beside the horse's shoulder during a series of back-up steps.

It's usually the case that as our precision improves, the horse's responses suddenly improve enormously. When we are consistently consistent, the horse begins to realize that our position and orientation are meaningful.

This exercise incorporates multi-signals* so that we end up having a variety of ways to communicate clearly.

We can begin this task using an open-ended lane. We want the horse comfortable standing in the lane before we close off the front. The horse is in the lane, the handler stays on the outside.

PREREQUISITES:
- Horse walks confidently between the handler and a fence or similar barrier.
- Horse understands a 'halt' signal.
- Handler easily slips into and out of 'zero intent' so the horse knows when he can relax in a 'wait' and when he is being asked to move. (See Chapter Three.)

ENVIRONMENT & MATERIALS:
- A work area where the horse is relaxed and confident.
- Ideally, the horse can see his buddies, but they can't interfere.
- The horse is not hungry.
- A lane into which the horse can walk comfortably but too narrow for him to turn around, with chest-high sides.
- Something safe to block off the front of the lane.
- For generalization, a safe corner e.g. a fence with an open gate or a fence with a barrier set at right angles to the fence.
- Halter and lead. A short (8') lead is easiest for teaching this task.

It's usually the case that as our precision improves, the horse's responses suddenly improve enormously.

I've used two green jump stands to block off the front of the lane. Now when we go into the lane, it makes sense to the horse to back out. In this photo the rope is lying over Boots' neck because we were weaning ourselves off dependence on the rope.

AIMS:
- A. Handler uses clear, consistent orientation, body language, gesture and voice 'back up' signals while staying shoulder-to-shoulder with the horse.
- B. Horse backs up staying shoulder-to-shoulder with the handler.
- C. Ideally the horse backs up in a straight line, but most horses find this hard because they naturally push off harder with one hind leg, which causes their hind end to drift over away from the stronger leg.

When we are consistently consistent, the horse begins to realize that our position and orientation are meaningful.

A ready-made corner with a fence and a gate.

CLIPS:

December 2018 Challenge BACK UP SHOULDER-TO-SHOULDER Clip 1.

December 2018 Challenge BACK UP SHOULDER-TO-SHOULDER Clip 2.

SLICES:

Keep session very short, three repeats are plenty. We can fit mini-sessions like this in-between chores or other things we are doing with our horse.

Stay with each slice until both horse and handler are fluid*.

1. Set up a lane open at both ends and ask the horse to walk through the lane while the handler walks alongside the outside of the lane, staying in position beside the horse's shoulder. Click&treat for walking through the lane.
2. When 1 is ho-hum, ask the horse to halt in the lane; click&treat for the halt and take up a 'zero intent' position for a few seconds, then walk the

horse out of the lane, maintaining the shoulder-to-shoulder position.

Walk a few loops that bring you back to halt in the lane, earning a click&treat for each halt.

3. When 2 is smooth, block off the front of the lane and ask the horse to walk into the dead-end space and halt; click&treat.
4. Staying in the shoulder-to-shoulder position, hold the rope in the hand nearest the horse and lift it straight up into the air and jiggle it lightly, while also saying your 'back up' voice signal (hopefully previously taught in Chapter Eight). Click&treat at the first indication that the horse is shifting his weight backwards, or if he indeed steps back half a step or more.
5. Either after 4 is established, or at the same time as you do 4 above, add in a 'back' hand gesture signal. The one I have found most useful is to raise my outside hand about level with the horse's eye and gesture backwards with it as in the upcoming photo.

In the same way that music is made up of notes and the pauses between the notes, we have pauses between asking the horse to repeat the same task.

Staying shoulder-to-shoulder, I lift the lead rope straight up and jiggle it lightly as well as use my voice signal. I also raise my outside hand to the horse's eye level and gesture backwards with it. At the same time, I'm using body language as I begin to step backwards. The rope signal can be faded out as soon as the horse responds to the voice and gesture signals.

6. Gradually use the hand gesture and voice signals more and fade out the rope signal as soon as the horse responds easily to voice and gesture.
7. Remove the barrier at the front of the lane but keep everything else the same. Now you will ask the horse to halt in the lane; click&treat, relax, then back out even though he could walk out of the lane forwards.
8. If it feels right, lay the rope over the horse's neck and become precise about using only your voice and hand gesture signals. If you do use the rope, keep a non-influencing drape in it unless you are specifically using it <u>momentarily</u> to send a message by jiggling it straight upward.

9. Move away from the lane and do the task starting in a corner with a fence on the far side of the horse.
10. Set up a barrier out in the open with a ground rail at a right angle to it and ask the horse to back away from the barrier. You can put the rail on the far side of the horse or between you and the horse.

    You will be able to see whether the horse tends to veer right or left as he backs up. As mentioned earlier, this is natural because in most horses one hind leg pushes off more strongly than the other hind leg.
11. To consolidate the habit of backing in a straight line, spend many short sessions backing between two rails, starting with a short distance and gradually adding more rails to make it longer. Start with the rails about a yard or meter apart and when that is smooth, make the lane narrower.
12. Ask the horse to back shoulder-to-shoulder with you at liberty, first alongside a fence, between rails and eventually out in the open.

Once a task has been acquired and become fluid, we want to generalize it to as many situations as we can find or set up and maintain it regularly.

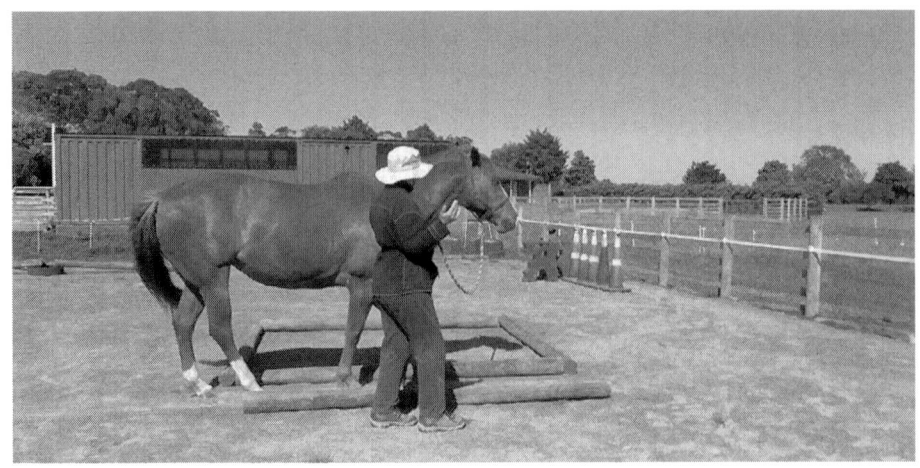

We walked through the lane of rails forward until her front feet were just past the rails, now we are backing up between the rails using hand gesture and voice signals.

GENERALIZATION:

The best generalization for this task is to do a tiny bit often and in as many different places as possible.

The end of the second video clip shows an extension task called, 'backing a square'. I ask for three or four steps back, then a 90-degree counter-turn, more steps back, counter-turn, more steps back, counter-turn until we have backed four sides of a square.

Asking the horse to back up while we face the same direction as the horse can be expended further. We can teach it:

- While standing beside the horse's ribs.
- Standing beside his butt.
- Standing behind him.

Once a horse understands the 'back' voice and gesture signals from behind, it becomes easy to invite him to exit a straight-load trailer.

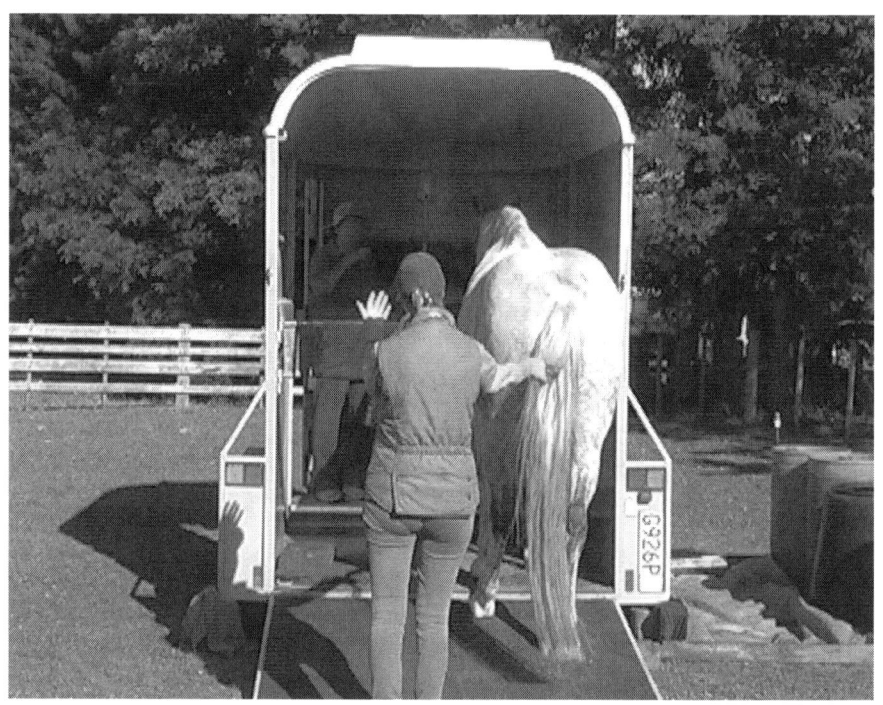

Bridget is using hand gesture and voice signals, plus touch signal on the tail, to ask Smoky to quietly exit the trailer.

Notes:

Notes:

Chapter Ten

Willing Whoa with a Voice Signal

INTRODUCTION:

It's great fun to refine a voice "Whoa" signal so that it works in a variety of situations. If we want to work on the halt, we will obviously also need our 'walk on' signals to be solid.

These two tasks are the foundation of pretty much everything we want a horse to do with us. Even teaching 'parking' starts with a solid, confident 'halt'.

Teaching the basic 'walk on' and 'halt' with precision is easiest when we are shoulder-to-shoulder with the horse. I like to teach 'halt' and 'walk on' with 'multi-signals'* or 'signal bundles'.

Using the multi-signals consistently at the beginning means that once the horse knows them well, I can use any one of them, or any combination of them, depending on what best suits the situation. The horse will also recognize the signals if I am walking beside his ribs or behind him (outside his blind spot).

The following two clips outline the 'walk on' and 'halt' multi-signals that we use. They are designed so that the touch signal on the halter via the lead rope quickly becomes unnecessary. The key is to keep all the other signals consistent. The added advantage is that once the multi-signals are well-established, we can use them to communicate at liberty.

CLIPS:

The clips give a solid explanation. The key points are in the next two photo captions.

Clip *#129 HorseGym with Boots* outlines the details of 'walk on'.

Clip #131 HorseGym with Boots outlines the details of 'halt'.

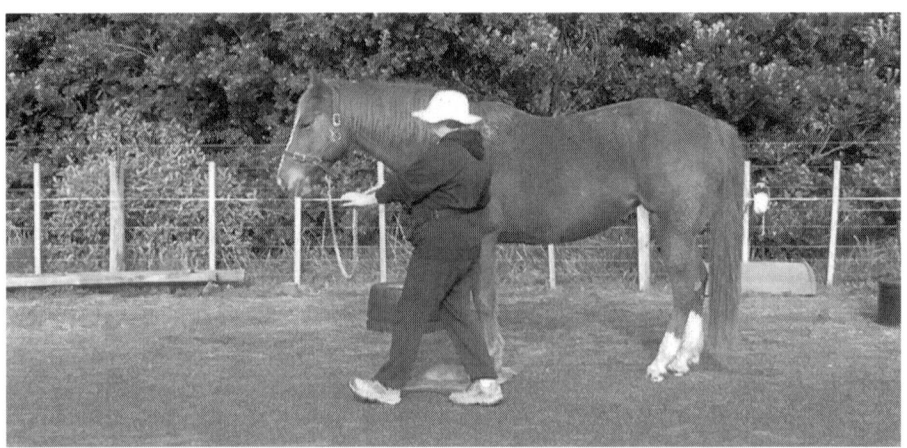

Our 'walk on' multi-signal: outside hand running up rope, breathing in, lifting torso, looking ahead, stepping forward with outside leg and saying 'walk on' all at the same time.

Our 'halt' multi-signal: slow down, breathe out, drop weight into hips as feet stop, raise rope slightly, and say, "Whoa", all at the same time.

PREREQUISITES:
- Handler has developed both 'walk on' and 'halt' multi signals.
- Horse responds willingly to 'walk on' and 'halt' signals.
- Horse is target-savvy and mat-savvy.
- The *20-Steps Exercise* in Chapter Six is also helpful.
- Decide on a consistent voice 'whoa' signal that does not sound like any of the other voice signals you use.

ENVIRONMENT & MATERIALS:
1. Work area where the horse is relaxed.
2. Ideally, the horse can see his buddies, but they can't interfere.
3. The horse is not hungry.
4. Depending on what you choose to do: halter and lead or safe enclosed area for working at liberty. A shorter 8 ft lead is easier to manage.
5. Buckets or tubs.
6. Familiar stationary nose targets.
7. Familiar mat targets.
8. Lunging or circle work gear if you use that option.

AIM:

To have the horse halt willingly and promptly in a variety of situations when he hears a voice 'whoa' signal.

Eventually we want the horse to be comfortable coming to a halt in unusual places.

GETTING STARTED:

The flow charts that follow shortly outline a variety of options we could use. To decide on a good starting point, do low-key experimentation with the horse to find out what he can offer already.

- Look through the flow charts and decide which route would be easiest for you and your horse to tackle first.

- Your first decision is whether you are going to use targets or teach without targets. You can easily add targets in strategic places but not use them all the time. While targets are often good to initially motivate the horse to try something, they can get in the way of refining a task.

- Decide if you will teach at liberty or with halter and lead. You can do some of each, whatever makes most sense to you and your horse. Some people don't have the facility to work easily and safely at liberty.

- Develop possible thin slices* for your chosen route before you start. My book, *How to Create Good Horse Training Plans* is full of information about how to develop your own Plans and Individual Education Programs*. Each horse and handler combination is unique. There is not a cookie-cutter method for teaching horses.

- Practice precision rope handling with a willing human if you have one. (See Chapter Seven.)

- Some of the tasks shown on the video clips, like backing up, recall, working on a circle or guiding the horse from beside his ribs, his butt and from behind, need a good level of proficiency before you add in 'Whoa'. The flow charts therefore cover an extensive sequence of learning if some of these things are new to your horse.

One starting point is to walk between mats or nose targets, using our voice 'whoa' signal just as the horse is about to stop anyway when he reaches the target. Once the voice 'whoa' signal is well established, we can check to see how well it works by asking for a halt between the targets, as illustrated in the video clips.

VIDEO CLIPS:

October 2018 Challenge: Voice Whoa Signal Clip 1.

This second clip introduces some of the generalizations and new contexts to which we can apply this skill. *October 2018 Challenge: Voice Whoa Signal Clip 2.*

This third clip links back to the *20 Steps Exercise* in Chapter Six. *October 2018 Challenge: Voice Whoa Signal Clip 3.*

THE FLOW CHARTS:

To use the flow charts, track a single route from left to right. When one sequence becomes ho-hum, chose another sequence and design a thin-sliced* plan for it.

For example, in the first video clip, I chose: STATIONARY TARGETS -- LIBERTY -- TUBS -- BESIDE NECK/SHOULDER -- TARGETS RELATIVELY CLOSE TOGETHER.

I modified it during the clip to walking beside Boots' ribs or butt, mainly because I couldn't yet walk very fast (new bionic knees) and she was keen to get to the next tub.

Notes:

Developing a Solid Voice "Whoa" Signal

USING STATIONARY TARGETS

- Whoa Between targets
- Targets Further apart
- Targets Close together
  - Beside neck or shoulder
  - Beside ribs
  - Beside butt
  - Behind horse
  - On a lunging circle
    - Reverse round pen (horse outside the pen barrier)
  - Facing front of horse
    - Backing up
    - Recall

Targets:
- Tub or bucket
- Stationary nose target
- Mat foot target

- Liberty
- Halter & Lead

A flow chart using targets showing various sequences we could set up to teach and generalize a willing, confident halt response to a voice signal.

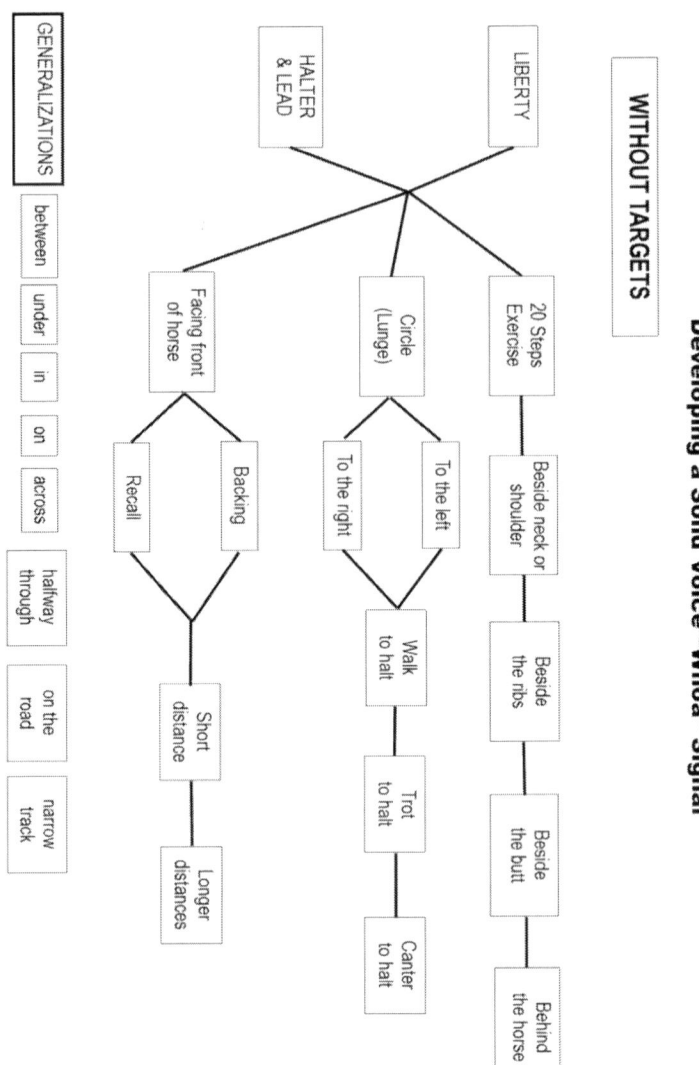

Flow chart showing possible training sequences for a willing halt with a voice signal without using targets.

GENERALIZATION:

The second video clip (*October 2018 Challenge: Voice Whoa Signal Clip 2*) illustrates some of the generalizations. As with everything we train, once a task has been acquired* and become fluid*, we want to generalize it to as many situations as we can find or set up. Plus, we want to ask for it frequently, so it settles into the horse's long-term memory.

Generalization means finding lots of new and unusual places to ask for 'whoa'.

One of my favorite generalization examples is from when I was long-reining Boots everywhere to establish long-reining firmly as part of our repertoire.

During an outing on a large farm with huge paddocks, we had to cross a stream. Usually the water was low enough for me to jump over without getting my feet wet. But on this day, I underestimated the depth of the water.

Boots willingly long-reined through the water in front of me. As I tried to leap over, I hit the water, lost my balance and dropped the reins. Boots kept on walking straight ahead. By the time I had pulled myself upright and out of the water, she was a good thirty meters away dragging the reins. I called out, "Whoooaaa", and she immediately stopped and waited for me to catch up with her.

It was a great outcome compared to a fright and panic run dragging reins through hilly terrain with open gates connecting several fields.

Walking together or long-reining out and about in the countryside brings its own challenges. A solid, well-practiced voice signal for 'Whoa' could well be the best thing we ever teach our horse.

We want to ask for a newly-learned task frequently, so it settles into the horse's long-term memory.

Chapter Eleven

Precision with a Rail

INTRODUCTION:

This challenge continues the attention we gave the 'halt' and 'walk on' in Chapter Six, includes shoulder-to-shoulder 'back up' (see Chapter Nine) and pays attention to careful use of zero intent* (see Chapter Three).

Synchronicity, moving fluidly together, is a cornerstone of horse behaviour. Whether horses are grazing as a group, walking together to water, or in flight due to a real or perceived danger, they remain tuned-in to each other's body language. Horses running full-flight in a group don't bump into each other.

As we become more precise, clear and consistent with our body language, we make it possible for our horse to read our intent clearly enough, so he can synchronize his movements to match ours. Sometimes we might want to match our movements to those of the horse.

The challenge in this task is to encourage handler and horse to move in unison using a single rail as the focal point.

When confusion arises, it's usually because our signals are not clear enough.

Boots at halt with her back feet just over the rail while I go to adjust the camera.

This exercise consists of five different tasks, but since we do them on the horse's left and right sides, they are actually ten tasks. Then we consolidate the tasks by doing them in at least two directions, giving us twenty tasks, or five tasks each of which has four variations.

Once all the tasks are going smoothly, we can mix them up in any order, which teaches us to be crystal clear for the horse and has the horse watch us carefully to stay in tune with our body language.

When confusion arises, it's usually because our signals are not clear enough. Clicker-savvy horses are usually super-observant of our body language as well as watching and listening for the voice and gesture signals we have taught them.

When we use the less dominant side of our body, it's common for our body language and gesture signals to be less precise than the ones we give with our dominant side. Once we become conscious of this stiffness on the side we don't use as much, we can work ·to improve our fluency* with body language and signals on that side.

It takes conscious practice to build new nerve-to-muscle connections, which is equally true for people and for horses.

Usually horses also have one side more flexible than the other. If the horse hasn't had much coaching on his right side, we have to be especially patient while he forms the nerve connections that enable smooth responses on his non-dominant side.

If a horse has been handled mostly on his left side, his right side may have 'right side neglect*'. Some horses with little or no experience of a handler on their right side, will also become concerned with this change of parameter*, showing 'right side anxiety*'.

If the horse has both 'right side neglect' and 'right side anxiety' it helps to set up an Individual Education Program* that teaches the beginning clicker training tasks on that side, as if teaching a new horse.

When I teach a series of moves like the ones in this chapter, I usually take a written memo card out with me, with a list of slices* outlining what I want to accomplish.

Some horses are, at first, not comfortable standing with an object under their belly, so before asking for a halt like this we would teach relaxed walking across a rail.

PREREQUISITES:

- Horse leads smoothly beside the handler's shoulder.
- Handler and horse agree on clear 'walk on', 'halt' and 'back up' signals while moving together shoulder-to-shoulder (see Chapter 9).
- These tasks may at first glance seem incredibly basic, but they are ideal for establishing secure two-way communication. You learn to communicate your intent with clarity. The horse communicates his willingness (or not) to follow the intent of your body language. He also communicates when he is relaxed with each slice and ready to tackle the next one.

ENVIRONMENT & MATERIALS:

- A work area where the horse is relaxed and confident.
- Ideally, the horse can see his buddies, but they can't interfere.
- Horse is not hungry.
- A rail; ideally one that will not 'roll' if the horse's foot nudges it. Half-round fence posts are ideal or put wedges under a round rail.
- Halter and lead or work at liberty in a safe enclosed area. A shorter 8 ft lead is easier to manage.
- When a horse is first learning these five tasks, one or two of them during one segment of a training session is plenty to start with. If we teach quietly with no fuss or drilling, the horse thinks about it and usually remembers what behaviors earned a click&treat during the previous session.
- It works best to do a little bit often.

AIMS:
- A. Handler improves his/her precision with 'walk on', 'halt' and 'back up' signals using a single rail as a focal point. Precision includes orientation, halt, walk-on and back-up body language as well as the timing of voice, gesture and touch signals.
- B. Handler uses his/her 'zero intent*' body language to build small pauses (dwell time*) into the work to encourage the horse to relax while waiting for the next set of signals.
- C. Horse develops confidence with:
    - Walking smoothly over a rail.
    - Standing with a rail under his belly.
    - Standing with a rail right in front of him.
    - Standing with a rail right behind him.
    - Backing over a rail.
    - His ability to correctly read his handler's body language.
- D. Horse places his feet carefully in response to handler signals.

Notes:

Once the horse understands these five tasks, he will watch carefully to stay in tune (in synchronicity) with us. Here we might next halt standing across the rail, halt after all four feet are over the rail or walk across the rail without stopping.

VIDEO CLIP:

This clip illustrates the slices outlined below. The numbered slices on the clip are <u>not</u> the same as the slice numbers below because in the video demonstration I carry out each task on both sides of the horse and in both directions.

August 2017 Challenge: PRECISION WITH A SINGLE RAIL.

SLICES:

- An option is to teach all five tasks smoothly staying on one side of the horse and then teach them again on the other side. Your horse will tell you which is best for him.
- Stay with each slice until it feels ho-hum for both of you, but work in short, relaxed sessions. We don't want to drill.
- After each click&treat, walk a circuit that brings you back to reset* the task.

1. Walk all four feet across the rail, halt a few paces beyond the rail, click&treat. Walk a circuit so you can again approach the rail from the same direction.
2. Halt with the rail under the horse's belly, click&treat; pause, walk on forward over the rail.
3. Halt before stepping over the rail, click&treat; pause, walk on over the rail.
4. Halt after all four feet have stepped over the rail, click&treat; pause, walk on.
5. Halt with the rail under the horse's belly, click&treat. Pause, ask the horse to back his front feet over the rail, click&treat; pause, walk on forward over the rail.
6. Repeat 1-5 approaching the rail from opposite direction or change the orientation of the rail.
7. Repeat 1-5 on the horse's other side if you have not already done each task on both sides.

GENERALIZATIONS:
1. Put the rail in different places.
2. Begin to chain some of the tasks together before a click and treat, as shown at the end of the first clip listed above.
3. Eventually, when the horse is ready, make your chain of tasks longer to include all five tasks in both directions over the rail before the click&treat.
4. Chain together all the tasks on both directions over the rail as in 2 above plus asking for them on both sides of the horse before the click&treat.
5. Add stepping all feet over the rail, halt, and back all four feet over the rail.
6. Set up multiple rails at various angles around your training area and do something different at each rail, or do the same thing at each rail.

7. Once your communication is well-established, do the rail tasks at liberty. It is usually most successful to work through the plan again from the beginning so if the horse is unsure about one of the slices, he can easily let you know so you can spend more time there. This clip illustrates: *August 2017 Challenge, LIBERTY PRECISION WITH A RAIL*
8. We can use a single rail for a few more 'precision exercises', as outlined in this clip: *July 2017 Challenge SINGLE RAIL PRECISION.*

   There is a companion clip where I did a self-assessment on the clip: *July 2017 Challenge ASSESSMENT.*

We are coming to a halt in front of the rail together. Some people like to train mostly at liberty. I like to use the halter and lead as lightly as possible to make a new task as clear as I can during the acquisition* stage. Then we check our fluidity* and consolidate at liberty.

If the horse gets confused at liberty, we back up a few slices and work through them again with halter and lead guidance.

If you begin with halter and lead, a nice way to ease into liberty is to work for a while with a neck rope. It's a good way to wean ourselves off reliance on a direct connection with the horse's head and depend more on our body language and gesture signals.

At first, we can attach a light lead to the neck rope, carrying it draped unless we use it momentarily to clarify our signal if the horse is unsure about our intent. Having only the neck rope on still allows us to gently remind the horse about the movement we will click&treat.

Some people like to teach as much as possible at liberty right from the beginning.

Use of a neck rope, first with a light lead attached, then by itself, is a good way to wean us off our reliance on halter and lead once the horse understands the tasks we are doing. We learn to rely more on our body language and gesture signals.

Notes:

Chapter Twelve

Changing Sides in Motion

INTRODUCTION:

When walking out and about with our horse, this task is a way of smoothly putting yourself between the horse and something coming up that he might find scary. Then if he leaps away sideways, he won't leap into you, so it is a great safety exercise.

It is also a horizontal flexion exercise. The task asks the horse to move in a semi-circle around the handler with flexion that encourages him to develop and maintain suppleness on both sides of his body.

If you do circle work on the lunge, inside a round pen or with the horse on the outside of a round pen, it is also a way to smoothly change the horse's direction. If you do Horse Agility, it is an easy way to set up for the best approach to the next obstacle.

This work encourages the handler to become ambidextrous*, able to give clear, precise, signals with both the right and left sides of the body. At the same time, we help the horse become more ambidextrous.

When we use the less dominant side of our body, it's common for our body language and gesture signals to be less precise than the ones we give with our dominant side.

Boots was walking on my right side. To begin the 'changing sides' task, I ask her to move in an arc in front of me toward my left side.

PREREQUISITES:

- Horse responds willingly to 'walk on' and 'halt' signals in a relaxed manner. (See Chapter Six.)
- Horse responds to soft rope signals. (See Chapter Seven.)
- Handler is adept at letting the rope out smoothly and collecting it in smoothly without losing the drape in the rope. It works well to practice this first with a dog on a long cord or another person standing in for the horse.
- Handler clearly moves into and out of 'zero intent*' so the horse knows when he can relax in a 'wait' and when he is being asked to move. (See Chapter Three.)

To complete the task from the photo above, I step forward as Boots comes around on my left side, to give her space to slot her shoulder alongside my left shoulder. We have changed sides and are still walking in the same direction.

ENVIRONMENT & MATERIALS:

- A work area where the horse is relaxed and confident.
- Ideally, the horse can see his buddies, but they can't interfere.
- The horse is not hungry.
- Halter and lead. A lightweight 10-12-foot lead rope makes it easier to keep a soft drape in the rope as the horse moves out and around.

AIMS:

A. Handler uses clear, consistent orientation, gesture and voice signals.

B. The horse understands the task to move forward away from us in order to walk an arc in front of us, then moves around so he can slot in beside our shoulder on our other side.

C. We can change sides plus change direction.

VIDEO CLIP:

June 2018 Challenge: CHANGING SIDES IN MOTION.

A) Changing sides and maintaining the same direction

SLICES:
1. Start by walking together shoulder-to-shoulder.
2. Hold the rope, with a non-influencing drape (smile), in the hand nearest the horse.
3. Slow your steps and at the same time, reach across your body with your outside hand to pick up the rope and put a directional signal on the rope to ask the horse to move forward and around you in an arc.
4. Be sure to let the rope flow smoothly through your hands as he moves out and around, so it doesn't tighten.
5. As he starts to turn on your other side, gently gather up the rope and walk forward so he has room to slot himself into position on your other side.
6. If you started with the horse on your left, he will now be on your right, and vice versa. Done elegantly, you will still be walking in your original direction.

Synchronicity with other horses is a fundamental horse behavior.

Boots was walking on my left side. Now she is moving in an arc in front of me toward my right and I'm taking a step forward, so she has space to slot in on my right side.

The series of photos coming up helps clarify the sequence of events.

Notes:

The four main parts of changing sides without changing direction.

B) Changing sides and direction

SLICES:

Note: For this task, the horse basically stays on the same side, but the handler turns to face the opposite direction, which means the horse is now on the handler's other side.

1. Start by walking together, shoulder to shoulder.
2. Pause and turn 90° to face the horse's neck/shoulder. At the same time, ask the horse to yield his hind end away from you.

3. Step back slightly and turn another 90° so you are walking in the opposite direction.

4. As you turn, ask him to swing his shoulder over into the space where you were. As he does, slot yourself along his other side and walk forward together.

5. You'll now be walking in the opposite direction with the horse on your other side.

Sequence of movements to change direction of travel as well as change the horse to my other side.

This can become a handy little warm-up exercise to check the horse's flexibility to the right and the left.

Notes:

Chapter Thirteen

Precision Leading Using 'Gates'

INTRODUCTION:

As mentioned in Chapter Eleven, synchronicity is a fundamental horse behavior. Horses stay in visual contact and move together. A warning snort by one horse will immediately alert all other horses who hear it. One horse startled into action will immediately be joined by the rest of his group.

It's possible for us to use this incredible sensitivity if we train ourselves to become clearer and more consistent with our body language. Once a horse realizes that our body language can be significant for him, he tends to watch it closely. If we go about improving our body language systematically, we can reap the benefit when we lead our horse.

We inevitably need to lead our horses from A to B. This task builds on the *20-Steps Exercise* in Chapter Six, the *Soft Response to Rope Signals* exercise in Chapter Seven and the backing-up exercises in Chapters Eight and Nine.

We might be leading our horse:

- Between paddocks.
- Between stable and paddock.
- Into and out of stalls.
- To and from our training area.
- Along a road or track for a walk.
- Alongside other horses.
- On the uneven road verge or ditch if big or unusual traffic comes along.
- Through gates of varying width.
- Through a narrow space.
- In a new area the horse has not seen before.

- Into a familiar area which suddenly has new things in it.
- Up and down slopes.
- Around obstacles.
- Through water.
- Across ditches or gullies.
- Into and out of a truck or trailer.
- Around a vet facility.
- Between cars and horse trailers.
- Past or among strange horses and strange people.
- Past pigs or donkeys or other animals unfamiliar to the horse.
- Past aggressive dogs.
- If we take our horse for walks, we may be in bush or forest with logs to step over, water to cross, other trail users to meet and pass.
- If we trail ride, we may have reason to dismount and lead the horse in narrow, unusual and sometimes dangerous places with poor footing.

I'm sure this is not an exhaustive list, but it makes the point that it is definitely in our interest, and in the horse's interest, to make precision leading exercises part of our horse's repertoire.

The 'gates' in this exercise are pairs of markers set up in a random pattern. The task is to organize the approach to each gate, so the horse can navigate it fluidly. We start with the gates well spread out and roomy to walk through.

Once a horse realizes that our body language can be significant for him, he tends to watch it closely.

I've set up seven gates so I can refine my body language for changes of direction as well as engage Boots in a gymnastic suppling exercise. Some gates are narrower than others. To begin with, make them all wider than the ones in this photo.

PREREQUISITES:

- Horse responds willingly to 'walk on' and 'halt' signals in a relaxed manner. (See Chapter Six.)
- Horse responds to soft rope signals. (See Chapter Seven.)
- Horse backs up willingly with the *'finesse back-up'* (Chapter Eight) and/or *'shoulder-to-shoulder back-up'* (Chapter Nine).
- It's a help if the horse understands the 'around' voice signal for turning as in the *figure 8 exercise* near the end of Chapter Six.

ENVIRONMENT & MATERIALS:

- A work area where the horse is relaxed and confident.
- Ideally, the horse can see his buddies, but they can't interfere.
- The horse is not hungry.

- Halter and lead. A shorter 8-foot lead makes it easier to keep a soft drape in the rope.
- A series of five or more gates made with pairs of markers such as cones, tread-in posts, pieces of firewood, rocks, containers of water (5-liter plastic containers are especially useful), barrels, jump stands, rags - anything that is safe to use.
- Each time we set up this exercise, we can put the gates in a different configuration. The number of gates is only limited by the size of the training area.

AIMS:
- A. Handler uses clear, consistent orientation, gesture, voice and halter-touch signals that allow the horse to smoothly navigate through each gate.
- B. Horse begins to seek out the next gate by reading the handler's body language and gesture signals.
- C. Clear communication for:
   - Walk on through the gate.
   - Halt between the 'gate' markers.
   - Halt and back through the gate.

VIDEO CLIP:

#158 HorseGym with Boots: PRECISION LEADING

SLICES:
- Very short frequent sessions work best. Stay with each slice until it feels ho-hum to both of you.
- Before asking the horse to negotiate the gates, walk through them yourself and visualize the order in which you will ask the horse to do them. Also explore the best way to approach each gate from various

directions. The less hesitancy in your actions, the easier it will be for the horse to read your intent*.
- Set out five or more gates well spread out, with a good-sized gap for each gate so it is easy for the horse to walk through.

1. Walk to each gate in turn and ask the horse to halt between the markers; click&treat each halt. If he wants to stop to sniff and investigate any of the markers, allow him all the time he needs to satisfy his curiosity. Wait with zero intent* for an 'okay to proceed*' signal (Chapter Four). In this situation, the 'okay' signal is when the horse brings his attention back to you. He may also sigh or breath out audibly.
2. When 1 is smooth, halt in every second gate you come to; click&treat.
3. When 2 is smooth, halt in every third gate you come to: click&treat.
4. As the horse shows he is ready to do more, carry on adding one more gate before the halt followed by click&treat, until you can do a whole series with one click&treat at the end of the series.
5. When 4 is good on one side of the horse, start again with slice 1 on the other side of the horse.
6. When 4 and 5 feel smooth and light, ask the horse to back up two or three steps after a halt in a gate. Work up to a series of occasional 'halts followed by a back-up', in-between walking forward through the gates.
7. Mix up:
    - Walking straight through gates.
    - Halting in a gate and walking on.

- Halting in a gate and backing up.

We can mark out gates using anything safe and handy. Here Boots and I are just coming to a halt between two cones.

Click&treat each halt. You can vary the halt to have the front feet between the markers, the horse in the center of the markers, or the hind feet at the markers as in this photo. It gives us a clear exercise to practice using our 'halt' signal with precision.

As Boots walks through one gate, I am already swiveling my body axis away from her to indicate that we are going to turn left to reach the next gate, not move to the one straight ahead. With practice, accurate timing of our body language becomes easier and the horse will read our intent more clearly. Note that the rope is held loosely, and I try to maintain a drape in it all the time so that the communication emphasis is on my body language and my voice signal which is, "Around".

As Boots walks through this gate, I am already turning my body axis toward her to indicate that we are going to make a counter-turn heading to the right after clearing the gate. If my plan was to go straight ahead, my shoulders would be square with the horse's shoulders.

I've asked Boots to halt and am now asking her to back up with body language, a gesture signal with my outside hand, as well as my voice signal for backing. In this photo I am working on her right side.

GENERALIZATIONS:

1. Make some or all the gates narrower.
2. Put the gates closer together.
3. Change the angle of the gates to each other.
4. Use different materials to create the gates.
5. Gradually introduce longer and variable 'wait' times after a halt in a gate.
6. Walk into or beyond the gate and ask the horse to back through it.
7. Add rails to some or all the gates, either on the ground or raised if you want to encourage hock flexion.
8. Work at liberty.
9. Set the gates out in different venues.
10. Add segments of trotting between or through gates.
11. Have the horse work with a different handler who trains the same way you do.

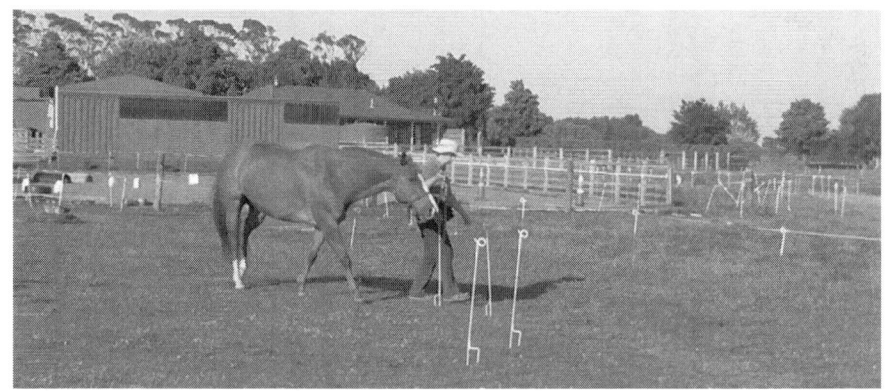

If we are working on grass, tread-in posts are handy to create gates.

Here we have added a rail to a gate and I'm using the 'finesse back-up' to ask Boots to back out of the gate rather than proceed forward.

The less hesitancy in our actions, the easier it will be for the horse to read our intent and match our movements.

Different venue and different markers.

When it all feels smooth with halter and lead, it's fun to see what the horse will offer at liberty. My body orientation shows that we are walking straight ahead for a few steps. During this session, Boots stayed with me for six gates, then wandered off.

The way we first present new material to the horse is crucial.

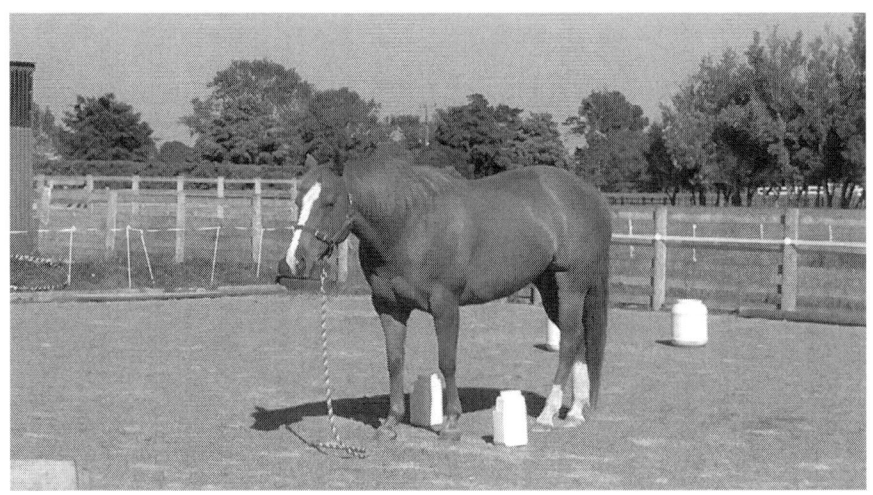

We can use the halt between the markers as another parking spot where we can gradually increase the 'wait' duration.

Notes:

Notes:

Conclusion

The Training Plans* outlined in this book hopefully present ideas that aid the development of handler precision with body language, gesture, touch and voice signals.

When we become clear and calm for our horse, he has reason to become more relaxed and willing to engage and move with us in a synchronized fashion.

Our aim is always to thin-slice* complex tasks into slices small enough so we can keep the horse continually successful (i.e. earn his next click&treat) until he can carry out the whole task, or do a task with more duration, with one click&treat at the end.

The more we tune in to the sensitive and observant nature of a horse, the more effective our training will be once we have him relaxed in our training environment.

All good training is geared to making the horse's life easier because it helps him to understand the restrictions placed on a life in captivity.

The more we can use positive reinforcement to teach him the things we want or need him to do, the more the horse will buy into our training sessions.

Some people try to use only positive reinforcement, but in my opinion that is like using only half the brain. Whole-brain horsemanship suggests that while we want to use positive reinforcement as much as possible, horses are more than astute enough to work with both positive and carefully thought-out negative (release) reinforcement.

The key to horse-friendly negative reinforcement is to keep our signal pressure (intent, gesture, touch) as light as possible - releasing it the instant the horse has responded.

Some tasks can be taught by using free-shaping*, adding signals once the horse is already doing the task we want.

Some tasks are grasped more easily by the horse if we use guided shaping*. We let the horse know precisely what will earn the next click&treat with one or more of:
- A direct touch.
- A clear gesture.
- A touch on the halter via a rope.

Many tasks make sense to the horse more quickly if we build them using an earlier skill such as following nose targets, or parking on foot targets.

There is no 'one size fits all'.

A review on Amazon is always appreciated.

Notes:

APPENDIX: List of YouTube Video Clips

Most of the video clips are shorter than five minutes, so they are quick to watch and easy to review if you are interested in specific tasks.

You can find my YouTube channel with a search for *Hertha MuddyHorse*. Relevant video clips were mentioned throughout the book. The clips are kept short for easy viewing and quick revision.

These PLAYLISTS mainly relate to the ideas in this book:

1. <u>Obstacle Challenges for Clicker Trainers</u>: the items in this playlist are dated with the month they were produced. They were first published on my Facebook page with the same name, but things rapidly get 'lost' there. Many of the clips for the book are in this playlist.

2. <u>HorseGym with Boots</u>: these are numbered. For example, if you would like to view Clip #132, simply put "*#132 HorseGym with Boots*" into the YouTube search engine and it should take you there. Each title starts with hashtag followed by its number.

3. <u>Starting Clicker Training:</u> contains clips about first starting out with clicker training.

4. <u>Free-Shaping</u>: These clips only have names. To find one, click on the playlist and scroll down to find the title that you want.

5. <u>Thin-Slicing</u>: These clips also only have names so please scroll down the list to find the title you want to view.

A list of all the current *Obstacle Challenges for Clicker Trainers* and *HorseGym with Boots* Clips follows, as well as titles in the *Free-Shaping* and *Thin-Slicing* examples.

Playlist: Obstacle Challenges for Clicker trainers

July 2017 Challenge Single Rail Precision
August 2017 Challenge Precision with a Single Rail
August 2017 Challenge Precision with a Single Rail at Liberty
September 2017 Challenge Figure 8
September 2017 Challenge Figure 8 at Liberty
October 2017 Challenge Park and Wait
November 2017 Challenge Mat Madness
December 2017 Challenge 20 Steps Exercise
January 2018 Challenge Begin Body Targeting
February 2018 Challenge Simple Recall Pt 1
February 2018 Challenge Simple Recall Pt 2
March 2018 Challenge Backing Up Part 1
March 2018 Challenge Backing Up Part 2
April 2018 Challenge Yield the Shoulder
May 2018 Challenge Yield Hindquarters
June 2018 Challenge Changing Sides in Motion
July 2018 Challenge One Step at a Time
August 2018 Challenge Head Down Building Duration
September 2018 Challenge Soft Rope Response Clip 1
September 2018 Challenge Soft Rope Response Clip 2
September 2018 Challenge Soft Rope Response Clip 3
September 2018 Challenge Soft Rope Response Clip 4
October 2018 Challenge Voice Whoa Signal Clip 1
October 2018 Challenge Voice Whoa Signal Clip 2
October 2018 Challenge Voice Whoa Signal Clip 3
November 2018 Challenge Sidestepping Clip 1
November 2018 Challenge Sidestepping Clip 2

November 2018 Challenge Sidestepping Clip 3

November 2018 Challenge Sidestepping Clip 4

December 2018 Challenge Shoulder to Shoulder Back Up

Playlist: HorseGym with Boots Series

Topics are added to this series as they are created.

1. Introduction
2. Giving meaning to the click
3. Stationary nose targets
4. Parking at a nose target (also spooky new things to touch)
5. Putting behavior 'on cue'
6. Foot targets (also, free-shaping new behavior)
7. Backing up from the mat
8. Duration on the mat
9. Putting the mat target 'on cue'
10. Generalizing mats
11. Mat-a-thons
12. Chaining tasks
13. Anthem is new to nose targets
14. Anthem is new to foot targets
15. Parking at a distance
16. The 'triple treat'
17. 'Walk-on' and 'halt' multi-cues
18. Parking out of sight
19. Free-shaping
20. The 'art of standing still'
21. Walk away for confidence (with new things)
22. Rope relaxation
23. Hosing on the mat (recognizing 'click points')
24. Parking commotions
25. Parking with ball commotion
26. 8 Leading Positions overview
27. Good Backing = Good Leading
28. Leading Position Three (beside neck or shoulder)
29. Leading Position Three with a 'circle of markers'

30. Leading Position Three duration exercise
31. Natural and Educated body language signals
32. Sensitivity to Body language
33. Opportunity, Signals 1
34. Signals 2: Gestures
35. Signals 3: Touch
36. Signals 4: Verbal signals (also environmental signals, horse-initiated signals and marker signals)
37. Signals 5: Intent
38. Signals 6: Body Orientation (of handler)
39. Train with a Lane 1
40. Train with a Lane 2
41. Leading Position Seven Clip 1 of 4, in front facing horse
42. Leading Position Seven Clip 2 of 4
43. Leading Position Seven Clip 3 of 4
44. Leading Position Seven Clip 4 of 4
45. Leading Position One: Clip 1 of 2 in front, facing away
46. Leading Position One Clip 2 of 2
47. Leading Position Two (horse's nose stays behind handler's shoulder)
48. Leading Position Eight Clip 1 of 7, Go, Whoa & Back (facing the horse's side)
49. Leading Position Eight Clip 2 of 7, Groom, Saddle, Relax
50. Leading Position Eight Clip 3 of 7, Drive-by Grooming & Mounting Prep
51. Leading Position Eight Clip 4 of 7, Side Step in Motion
52. Leading Position Eight Clip 5 of 7, Yielding Front End & Hind End
53. Leading Position Eight Clip 6 of 7, Side Step from Halt
54. Leading Position Eight Clip 7 of 7, Arc Exercise
55. Leading Positions Four and Five (beside ribs & beside butt)
56. Leading Position Four, Clip 2
57. Leading Position Six Clip 1 of 8, Liberty (behind horse)
58. Leading Position Six Clip 2 of 8, One long rein

59. Leading Position Six Clip 3 of 8, Square of lanes
60. Leading Position Six Clip 4 of 8, Rope Calmness
61. Leading Position Six Clip 5 of 8, Two Long Reins: Circle & Weaving
62. Leading Position Six Clip 6 of 8, 4 Leaf Clover Exercise
63. Leading Position Six Clip 7 of 8, 'Gates', Guided Rein, Obstacles
64. Leading Position Six Clip 8 of 8, Trailer Prep
65. Haltering process (with guided free-shaping)
66. Importance of Clear Signals
67. Prep 1 for Weaving, 90 and 180 degree turns; 'Draw' and 'Drive'
68. Weave Prep 2, 360 degree turns
69. Weave Prep 3, Weave a series of objects
70. Weave Prep 4, Only the horse weaves
71. Weave Prep 5, Curves, Circles, at Liberty
72. Ground-tie Clip 1, Getting Started
73. Ground-tie Clip 2, Another Venue
74. Thin-slicing a Trailer Simulation
75. Quiet Sharing of Time and Place
76. Active Sharing of Time and Place + Greet & Go
77. Claim the Spot
78. Watchfulness First Action
79. Watchfulness Second & Third Actions
80. Guiding from Behind
81. Shadow Me
82. Boomerang Frolic
83. Shadow Me Duration with Clicker Training
84. Shadow Me Using Targets
85. Walk On, Halt, Back-up
86. Mats & One Step at a Time
87. Relaxation with Body Extensions
88. Foot Awareness
89. Balance on 3 Legs
90. Walk Around to Each Foot
91. Clean All Feet from One Side
92. Hoof Stand Confidence
93. Spray Bottle Confidence
94. Loose Rope Leading
95. Backing Down Slopes
96. Tying Up

97. Single Steps Forward and Back
98. Parking Ground Tied
99. Noise Nonsense
100. Butt Bingo
101. Using Mats for Trailer Loading
102. Send Horse to Nose Target
103. Trailer Loading Mini-Skills
104. Trailer Simulation 1
105. Trailer Simulation with Dead End
106. Unusual Surfaces for Trailer Loading
107. Trailer Entry & Exit Facing the Horse
108. Butt Bar Simulations for Trailer Loading
109. Real Trailer Intro
110. Outside the Trailer
111. Simulation Beside the Trailer
112. Playing with the Ramp
113. Into the Trailer
114. Follow the Target into the Trailer
115. Mat Targets into the Trailer
116. Tests for Butt Bar Readiness
117. Fun Trailer Stuff
118. Relaxation Checks
119. Unusual Surfaces with Bottles
120. Water as Unusual Surface
121. Stick & Rope Confidence
122. Counting
123. Walk On & Halt with Mat
124. Free-Shaping Mat Targets
125. Nose Target Bingo Game
126. The Trailer (playing outside and inside the trailer mostly at liberty)
127. Liberty Loading
128. Thin-Slicing the Tunnel
129. 'Walk on' Multi-Signals
130. Targeting Body Parts
131. 'Halt' Multi-Signals
132. Halt & 'Walk on' with Mats
133. Getting Behind the Horse
134. Tossing the Rein from Behind
135. Halt in the Lane
136. Body Extension Tap Signals
137. Turn Voice Signals

138. More Voice Turn Signals
139. One Long Rein, Right Side
140. One Long Rein, Left Side
141. Smoky on a Single Rein
142. Soft Yield to Rein – 1
143. Soft Yield to Rein – 2
144. Soft Yield to Rein – 3
145. Soft Yield to Rein – 4
146. Smoky Learns about Two Long Reins
147. Smoky in New Places
148. Backing Up
149. Weaves and Circles
150. Direction Skills
151. Obstacle Circuits
152. Generalization of Long-reining Skills
153. Zero intent and Intent
154. Okay to Repeat Signals; Ear and Belly Rubbing
155. Okay to Repeat Signals; Tooth Inspection
156. Okay to Repeat Signals; with a Nose Target
157. Okay to Proceed Signals; with a Mat
158. Precision Leading with 'Gates'

Playlist: Thin-Slicing Examples

This playlist includes thin-slicing examples about the following topics. To find a specific clip, go to the *Thin-Slicing Examples* playlist in my channel and scroll down to find the one you want. New clips are added as they are made.

- Tunnel with Boots
- Pool Noodle task
- Head Rocking for Poll Relaxation
- Bottle Bank obstacle
- Zigzag for Horse Agility
- Yield Shoulder into a Turn on the Haunches
- Stepping over rails
- Soft yield to Rein Signals (5 Clips which also have their own Playlist)

- Thin-slice *'The Box'* Movement (back, sideways, forward, sideways)
- Backing up
- Rope Texting
- Thin-slicing the 1m board
- Water & Tarp obstacle
- Thin-slice the 'Shadow Me' Game at Liberty
- Free-shape Learning to Ring a Bell
- Back Up to Mounting Block

Playlist: Free-Shaping Examples

This playlist includes clips using the free-shaping technique to teach a task. To find a particular clip, go to the *Free-Shaping Examples* playlist in my channel and scroll down to find the clip you want. Most of these clips show both free-shaping and thin-slicing.

- Table Manners for Clicker Training
- Boots and Bicycle
- Bob meets Bicycle (Bob is a young quarter horse)
- Introduction to a saddle (with Bob, his first meeting with a saddle)
- Head-lowering (2 Clips)
- Clicker 1 with Smoky
- Smoky and Dumb-bell target
- Boots picks up the Dumb-bell
- Free-shape Learning to Ring a Bell

There are also short playlists on specific topics including:

- Thin-slicing the Wagon-wheel obstacle
- Teaching the S-bend
- Soft Yield to Rein Signals (5 clips)
- Hula Hoop Challenges (5 clips)
- Single Obstacle Challenges
- 2012 Horse Agility

- 2014 Horse Agility
- 2015 Horse Agility
- 2016 Horse Agility
- 2017 Horse Agility

Most of the Horse Agility clips have a commentary explaining the tasks and showing where we lost marks. Each task is marked out of ten, five points for the handler and five points for the horse. Some are at liberty and others are with halter and lead.

If you are interested in Horse Agility, the club is at **www.thehorseagilityclub.com.**

Reference List

Abrantes, Roger. DVDs (2013). *The 20 Principles all Animal Trainers Must Know.* Tawzer Dog LLC. www.TawzerDog.com

Bruce, Georgia. www.clickertraining.org

Camp, Joe (2011). *Training with Treats: with relationship & basic training locked in, treats can become an excellent way to enhance good communication.* 14 Hands Press; USA.

De Waal, Frans (2005). *Our Inner Ape: A leading primatologist explains why we are who we are.* Riverhead Books; New York.

Draaisma, Rachaël. (2018). *Language Signs & Calming Signals of Horses: Recognition and Application.* CRC Press; Boca Raton, Florida.

Foley, Sharon. (2007). *Getting to Yes: Clicker training for improved horsemanship.* T.F.H. Publications Inc.; Neptune City, NJ, USA.

Hanson, Mark. (2011). *Revealing Your Hidden Horse: a revolutionary approach to understanding your horse.* www.amazon.com

Hogan, Peggy. (2018). Facebook page: https://www.facebook.com/groups/ClickerTrainingHorses/

James, Hertha. (2017). *Conversations with Horses: An In-depth look at the Signals & Cues between Horses and their Handlers;* www.amazon.com.

James, Hertha. (2017). *Walking with Horses: The Eight Leading Positions;* www.amazon.com.

James, Hertha. (2017). *How to Create Good Horse Training Plans: The Art of Thin-Slicing;* www.amazon.com.

Karrasch, Shawna. (2012). *You Can Train Your Horse to do Anything! On Target™ Training: Clicker training and Beyond.* www.amazon.com

Kurland, Alexandra. (2005). *The Click That Teaches; Riding with the Clicker.* The Clicker Center; Delmar, New York.

Pavlich, Leslie. (2008). *Clicker Training: Colt Starting the Natural Horse.* (Amazon On-Demand Publishing; www.amazon.com

Pryor, Karen. (1999). *Don't Shoot the Dog: the new art of teaching and training.* Bantam; New York. {About much more than dogs.}

Pryor, Karen. (2009). *Reaching the Animal Mind: Clicker training and what it teaches us about all animals.* Scribner; New York.

Pryor, Karen. (2014). *On My Mind: reflections on animal behavior and learning.* Sunshine Books Inc.; Waltham, MA, USA.

Schneider, Susan M. (2012). *The Science of Consequences: how they affect genes, change the brain and impact our world.* Prometheus Books; New York.

Wilsie, Sharon & Gretchen Vogel. (2016). *HorseSpeak: The Equine-Human Translation Guide; Conversations with Horses in their Language.* Trafalgar Square Books; North Pomfret, VT.

Glossary

Items with an asterisk (*) are also in the glossary.

Acquisition: The beginning phase of training something new. The handler has to work out a series of slices* that take the horse's behavior from a first approximation to the whole defined task done smoothly.

Ambidextrous: Able to carry out tasks smoothly with both the right and left sides of the body.

Anchor Behavior: This describes a simple task that we teach as a foundation for a more complex task. For example, to teach a horse to target his knees, forehead, ears, eye, hind legs, shoulder or hindquarters to my hand, I established the knee target as our anchor behavior. I taught it first to a high proficiency. Then, when I introduced the idea of targeting a different body part to my hand, I started with the well-known knee target and then suggested a different body part. The anchor behavior 'sets the stage' for the activity we are doing.

Behavior: That which is actually happening, not colored by our expectations or an emotional slant from our personal viewpoint.

Body Extensions: A general name for the sticks, whips, wands, reeds, strings, ropes, halters, reins, bridles, saddles and harnesses that people use with horses.

Body Language: the postures, orientations, energy levels and gestures that communicate intent to another being. It is the main language of horses.

Brainstorm: The act of writing down everything we can think of about a topic, without giving any of the ideas a value judgment until later. It often helps to do this over several days, so our mind can mull over the topic and come up with new ideas and new connections. We can ask other people to contribute their ideas. A thorough brainstorm is an ideal way to begin writing a detailed Training Plan* and an Individual Education Program*. We can use the mind mapping* format to lay out our brainstorm ideas.

Capturing: If we click&treat at the moment the horse does a behavior that we like, we can 'capture' the complete behavior*. For example, the first time a horse touches his nose to a target we are holding out to him, we click&treat to 'capture' the specific complete behavior of 'put your nose on this target'.

Other examples are click&treat for forward movement, backing up, following us, coming toward us, a stretching bow, pawing, rearing, lowering the head, transitions between gaits, ear position, relaxed body language. Once the horse links the behavior to the click&treat, we can add touch, gesture and voice signals to the behaviors if we want to be able to request them.

Capturing is ideal for adding naturally-occurring behaviors, or behaviors we can arouse with the horse's curiosity, into the horse's repertoire.

Chaining: Linking together a number of tasks where each one relates to the task that has gone before. For example, if we want to ride our horse with a saddle, we start with building confidence with a saddle pad. Then we might run a rope around the horse's girth, so we can tighten and loosen it to simulate a girth. Then we introduce the saddle, first as an object to explore, then on the horse's back.

When that is smooth, we add the girth, tightening it in easy stages while moving the horse between each new tightening. This chain would continue with teaching the horse to do ground exercises wearing the saddle, stand relaxed at a mounting block, be comfortable with our weight lying across the saddle, one foot in the stirrup, sitting on the horse, asking the horse to move by walking between familiar stationary targets or following a person on the ground, and so on.

Charging the Clicker: When we first introduce a marker sound followed by a food treat, the horse has no idea that the sound and food are connected. We 'charge the clicker' by pairing the sound with the treat until the horse understands that when he hears our distinct marker sound, a treat will follow. Ways to do this are outlined in Chapter One.

Click Point: The specific behavior* (or end of a behavior chain*) we are presently actively seeking to reward with a click&treat.

Clicker-Savvy: This describes a horse who understands the relationship between the marker* sound the trainer uses (e.g. the 'click') and the treat. The horse knows that when he hears the marker* sound, he has done the action (or inaction) that will earn the next treat.

Clicker Training: General name for training using the 'mark and reward' system. We can use a mechanical clicker, a tongue click*, a special word, or any special sound to **mark** the exact moment that the horse is doing what we want. The 'marker'* sound is immediately followed by a small food treat.

Click&treat: The 'click' marks the exact behavior we would like. The 'treat' follows immediately after the click. The horse will seek to repeat the behavior that produced the click followed by the treat. Clicker training is also called the 'mark and reward' system.

Comfort Zone: An animal's comfort zone is defined by all the places and activities with which they feel at ease. Everything that can be done without anxiety falls into the comfort zone. When working with a horse we have to be aware of his comfort zone at the moment, as well as our own.

Consistency: This is the backbone of all good training. The handler needs to be consistent with the signals, body orientation and energy levels he uses to express his intent* to the horse. Through consistency, the horse and handler can develop a clear private language between the two of them.

By being consistent, we build the horse's confidence that he can understand our meaning. Inconsistent handling leaves horses in mental and emotional turmoil, often causing them to switch off or express a desire to leave the situation.

Counter-Conditioning: This is the behavior biologist's term for pairing a desired outcome with something that normally causes an anxiety or fear response in a horse. Clicker training* allows us to make the outcome a desired food reward, which clicker-savvy* horses value highly unless they are unusually stressed.

For example, if a horse is anxious about a wheelbarrow, we can put the wheelbarrow in the horse's pen. Then we wait and observe; click&treat as the horse progressively looks at the wheelbarrow, approaches it, sniffs at it, and so on.

Walking on the road, we can click&treat at the approach of every vehicle. Done consistently, the horse will begin to recognize a wheelbarrow or vehicle as an opportunity to score a click&treat rather than something to worry about.

Counter-conditioning is gradually getting a horse used to something which is not part of a horse's normal life. It means breaking big tasks or expectations into small enough pieces (slices) which we can click&treat and gradually chain* together. In this way, we gradually build the horse's confidence with new experiences. It is a key part of desensitization*, habituation* and 'building confidence'.

Criteria: These are the expectations that we set for a specific lesson. For example, if we are teaching side-stepping, the expectation (criterion) for our first lesson may be to get a single sideways step with the forequarters or the hindquarters, at which point we click&treat. If that goes well, we may shift the expectation (criterion) for our next lesson to a sideways step with both front and hind ends before we click&treat, and so on until the horse easily does multiple sideways steps.

Desensitization: see 'Counter Conditioning' and 'Habituation'.

Dwell Time: The pauses we put between repeats of a task when we stand quietly with the horse and let him absorb the last part of the lesson. We can click&treat the act of standing quietly with the head forward (as opposed to nudging the treat pouch or pocket). We can look for relaxation signs such as: head lower than withers, breathing out or sighing, total body at ease, soft ears, eyes, nostrils, lower lip and tail. Sometimes we might click&treat for these signs of relaxation.

Emotional Neutrality: The handler's ability to stay calm and not 'buy into' any upset or excessive energy that the horse or people in the vicinity are showing. Horses are highly tuned-in to the emotional state of other horses and people nearby. If we can remain calm, the horse is able to link in to our calmness and relaxation. If we are nervous or fearful, the horse has no reason to feel comfortable with what we are asking him to do.

Feedback: Whatever the horse does is feedback that informs our decision about what to do next. Our own feelings about what is happening are also important feedback, since it is imperative that we stay in a calm, relaxed mental state while we are training. Whether feedback is positive, negative or neutral, it all has value.

Fluidity: The second phase of training which follows acquisition*. In this phase, frequent short practice sessions improve the way a task is carried out and put it into the horse's long-term memory.

Free-shaping: Rather than influencing the horse directly, free-shaping sets up a puzzle and allows him to solve it in his own time and in his own way.

For example, when we first introduce a tarp, we can put it out, wait, and observe in order to click&treat each slice of the horse's exploration of the new object: looking toward it, moving toward it, sniffing it, putting a foot on it, walking on it, and so on.

His motivation, (rather than application and release of signal pressure) is his natural curiosity and his instinctive seeking response to obtain more of what he likes (the treat that follows the click).

In other words, he has learned a new way to gain 'forage' from the environment, in this case, a treat from the handler for carrying out a specific action.

Another example: when I wanted Boots to feel comfortable moving beside my bicycle, I walked or rode it around the arena while she was at liberty, with a click&treat first when she looked at it, when she moved closer to it, when she sniffed it, when she followed along with it, and so on.

Generalization: The third phase of training, following Fluidity*, when we expand a task into new contexts and new venues.

Gregarious: Describes animals who prefer living together in groups.

Guided Shaping: Using touch or gesture to help the horse understand the movement we'd like him to do. As soon as the horse makes an attempt in the direction of what we want, we release the signal pressure plus click&treat. This way of training combines the best of release reinforcement* plus the best of reward reinforcement*.

Guided shaping is intimately related to the thin-slicing* of tasks. Its magic lies in immediate removal of the guiding pressure as soon as the horse responds in the way we want, plus a simultaneous click&treat.

Luring* is another example of guided shaping. Once the horse understands that putting his nose on a target will earn a click&treat, we may want to teach him to follow a hand-held target. We click&treat when the horse takes a step (and eventually many steps) to reach the target. Offering the target is the gesture.

We can then use guided-shaping to develop further behaviors*. We can ask the horse to follow a target to walk a circle, weave objects, turn, or stand still and bend his neck around to touch the target.

We can also use stationary nose targets and mats to shape a willingness to walk with the handler. The horse soon realizes that the handler will guide him to another place that earns a click&treat (or a nice patch of grass if out and about).

Having the horse keen to seek out a target opens a large range of training possibilities without the need for halters and ropes if we are in a safe, enclosed area.

Habituation: This is repeated low-key exposure to a new environment or situation so that over time an initial anxious response is no longer aroused. For example, if we feed a horse at his trailer for several days, then at the entrance to the trailer for several days, then halfway in the trailer for several days and then at the front of the trailer every day, the horse has the time and motivation to enter the trailer and exit the trailer when he finishes eating. Habituation is also often called desensitization or 'confidence building' and it is part of counter-conditioning*.

Individual Education Program (IEP): This is created by taking a general Training Plan* and refining it to suit the character type, age, health and background experience of the individual horse we are working with.

Additionally, the IEP considers all the same factors in the handler. For example, although I was athletic in my youth, bionic knees now set a limit to how fast and far I can move.

Inhibitors: Anything we do and use to keep ourselves, our horse and others around us safe. Inhibitors include fences, ropes and reins that keep the horse contained in a safe area. Inhibiting actions include the use of our arms and body extensions to block behaviors that may harm the horse, the handler or others.

We want to familiarize a horse with inhibitors such as ropes and body extensions while he is in his home environment. Then they will make sense to him if we have to use them in an unfamiliar environment.

Intent: Horses are masters at the art of reading the intent of another horse. If handlers are consistent with their body language and ways of focusing, horses usually quickly learn to respond to the intent of a gesture, a touch, projected energy or breathing rate. The message is conveyed by body language (sometimes including sound) and change in energy.

Horses raised with other normal horses learn to respond to tiny body language shifts such as the angle of an ear, the tilt of the head, the position of the neck, the smallest flick of the tail. They readily apply this body-language-reading skill to a trusted handler with consistent habits.

Horses hand-reared in the absence of other horses often lack the skills and etiquette of equine social interaction.

Learning Frame of Mind: To be ready to learn something, humans and horses need to be relaxed, well fed and watered, not needing to urinate or defecate, not be too hot or too cold and not be in pain. If we are anxious, fearful, too hungry, cold or hot, or distracted by something else going on, we are not in our comfort zone*.

Most of our brain space will be taken up with trying to regain our comfort zone. A horse with an adrenalin rush needs time to move and cavort until the adrenalin is used up and he's able to relax again. There will be times when the best way forward is to enable our horse to run off his excess energy.

If the exercise to be learned includes active gymnastic movements, we have to begin the session by warming up the muscles, so the horse is able to respond comfortably.

Luring: A) Putting a food reward in a position that motivates the horse into a new behavior; e.g. placing a treat on a tarp so the horse steps on the tarp, putting food in the trailer, laying out piles of hay so we can ask the horse to move between the piles.

B) Once the horse understands the concept of putting his nose or feet on a target to earn a click&treat, we can use targets as lures to ask a horse to walk patterns with us or to walk forward with us toward a fixed target.

Maintenance: The fourth phase of training, following Generalization*. If the task is not something we do regularly, we must ensure that we revisit it often enough to keep it in the horse's repertoire.

Markers: A marker is the specific sound we use to let a horse know he has done the action (or maintained the inaction) that earns a treat. The marker can be a short, clear word not commonly used, a tongue click, the click of a mechanical clicker, the sound of a specific letter of the alphabet or a short nonsense word like 'biff' or 'ubu'. The key is to use the sound with total consistency, so the horse knows without doubt what sound signals that a treat is coming. The reward, when clicker training horses, is usually a small food treat.

Mugging: When a horse tries to put his nose into our pocket or treat pouch. The very first task when starting clicker training is to teach the horse that a treat will only ever be delivered if he keeps his head away from the treats. (See Chapter One.)

Multi-signal: (Sometimes called a 'signal bundle') using a combination of two or more of: gesture, voice, touch, body language intent to indicate the behavior we would like from the horse.

If the horse knows a variety of signals for a certain behavior, we can use the one most appropriate in a specific situation. If the horse is unsure about what we are asking, we can add another signal from a familiar 'signal bundle' to clarify the situation for him.

We can use voice, gesture and body language signals to influence the horse at liberty, either for exercise, training or while doing chores in his company.

Negative reinforcement: Stopping an action the horse understands as a signal* or stopping an action he finds bothersome. The pressure* we apply to the horse motivates his action, but it's the prompt *removal* of the pressure that reinforces the horse's action because it tells him that what he did will remove the pressure.

Note: 'negative' is not used in the sense of being 'bad'. It is used in the mathematical sense of *subtracting* something (i.e. the signal pressure we have applied) from a situation. This is the most common type of reinforcement used by most horse trainers.

Okay Signals: These are sometimes called 'start buttons' and have a variety of other names. We look for an explicit 'okay' consent signal from the horse while working with stationary tasks such as confidence with a husbandry procedure.

We begin by introducing the task with a click&treat for an approximation of the task with which the horse remains comfortable/relaxed. Then we pause in zero intent* position and watch the horse closely for a sign that indicates he is okay for us to 'do it again'. It can take a while for the horse to establish a consistent 'Okay to Repeat' or 'Okay to Proceed' signal, or it might appear quickly.

Gradually we work (in thin-slices*) from the approximation the horse can give us to the final desired behavior; e.g. putting on a halter, lifting of lips for tooth inspection, turning of neck toward needle simulation with a toothpick, bringing eye to a cloth for cleaning or medication, accepting a worming tube. (See Chapter Four.)

Parameters: The guidelines we set up to work within. See also 'criteria'.

Positive reinforcement: When the horse does something we like, we highlight the moment with a marker* sound and promptly deliver a treat. The treat is something the horse loves to receive, usually a small tasty morsel.

We can tell whether an added treat is reinforcing if the horse begins to offer the behavior we want more frequently.

Note that the term 'positive' is used in the mathematical sense of *adding* something to the situation, in this case a marker sound and a treat.

Many people think that taking away their signal pressure* is the 'reward' and therefore they are using positive reinforcement. However, release of pressure is 'negative reinforcement' because the pressure has been removed (or *subtracted*) from the situation.

This misunderstanding has led to a great deal of confusion for people trying to do their best with their horses.

Pressure: It can be argued that almost everything people do with horses consists of some sort of pressure. As with stress, pressure is essential for anything to happen, but too much pressure (or stress) causes extreme anxiety and panic.

Arriving with a pocket or pouch full of treats is a form of pressure. It motivates the clicker-savvy horse to engage in working out what will result in click&treat right now.

Good horse training has clear goals, cuts a big task into its smallest clickable portions, teaches each portion or slice until they can all be chained* together with one click&treat at the end. Done this way, there is seldom need for much pressure other than a light guiding touch or gesture.

Prerequisites: Essential things the horse needs to know already, before we can expect him to confidently learn the new thing we want to teach.

Proprioception: An individual's ability to sense where his body parts are, as well as the amount of effort being used if they are moving. Varied physical activity across varied terrain increases this ability.

Protected Contact: Having a barrier between the horse and the handler, or having the horse tied up. Most clicker trainers use protected contact when they begin clicker training* or if they are with a horse they don't know well. Protected contact allows us to move away if the horse gets over-enthusiastic about food being part of his training.

Rate of Reinforcement: How often we click&treat. At the beginning of teaching something new, we use a high rate of reinforcement, sometimes as much as 20 treats in a minute. As the horse learns each additional slice* of a task, we move the click point* along to the end of the next slice, so the horse does a bit more before the next click&treat.

Once the horse understands all parts of a complex task, the click&treat usually follows completion of the whole task. In other words, as the horse becomes more proficient with a task, the rate of reinforcement naturally declines. However, it is important to always click&treat for a job well done.

A comparison to consider might be how long we would keep on doing a job if suddenly there is no payment on pay day or the resources we earn with our effort no longer arrive.

Reflex action: A term used for an instinctive response. It is something we or any animal does without thinking about it first. A reflex action can be to move 'away', like jerking our hand away when it touches something hot. Maybe our whole body jumps away when we see a big cockroach in our sock drawer.

Generally, reflex actions are concerned with physical safety. One good jolt from an electric fence can modify behavior around electric fences for a long time.

Horses, being prey animals, rely on flight for safety and have a strong set of instinctive responses. We need to be aware of these and recognize them for what they are: the natural reflex actions of a prey animal.

We can take the horse out of the wild, but we can't take their instinctive reflex actions out of them. We must incorporate them into the way we care for and train our horses.

Release reinforcement: Another name for 'negative reinforcement'* – removing (releasing) signal pressure* when we get the response we want.

Reset: When the horse is unsure about what we are asking, rather than 'correct' the horse, we quietly pause, count to five or ten, and set things up so we can start again. If the horse does not understand what we'd like him to do, we usually need to cut the task into smaller slices (the process of thin-slicing*).

The point of positive reinforcement training is that we organise the learning sequence so that the horse can be continually successful (i.e. easily earn his next click&treat).

We do nothing that makes the horse feel wrong or lose confidence, because obviously we have not yet shown him clearly enough what we want, so he can't actually be 'wrong'. There is always the possibility that he is having an off-day or has pain somewhere. Keeping the horse's confidence is always more important that accomplishing a task right now.

Reward reinforcement: Another name for 'positive reinforcement'* – adding the marker sound* and treat reward when we get the response we want.

Right-side anxiety: If a horse has always been handled on his left side, he won't be used to a handler asking him to do things on his right side and he may show signs of stress about things that he does perfectly well when the handler in on his left side. (See also right-side neglect.)

Right-side neglect: If a horse has not been trained to accomplish all tasks asked of him on both sides of his body, the seldom-used side (usually the right) will not have formed strong nerve pathways from brain to muscle. It is up to the handler to spend time on either side of the horse until both sides feel equal.

As humans are right or left-handed, so horses usually use one side of their body more than the other and fall into the habit of doing so. It takes effort and practice to become ambidextrous* because only repeated specific movement will form the new nerve pathways needed to become fluent*.

Shaping: When we want to teach something, we experiment to see what the horse can offer already. Then we carefully develop an Individual Education Program* which allows us, using very small steps (slices), to influence the horse's behavior until he can confidently carry out the total task we want to accomplish.

All interaction with a horse shapes his behavior*, whether we intend it to or not. How he is kept and fed also shape his behavior.

Signal pressure: Whenever we show up and want the horse to do things with us, we are exerting signal pressure. The pressure can become an extremely light message of communication once the horse understands what we want.

In some circumstances, the pressure will be more intense if we need to clarify a message or if safety is our first concern.

As mentioned earlier, turning up with treats is signal pressure too, since it communicates the expectation that we will be rewarding specific behaviors.

Slices: A slice is the smallest noticeable bit of behavior toward completion of a task we want to accomplish, that we can click&treat*. The process of thin-slicing* lets us lay out a possible sequence of these 'bits of behavior' that might make sense to the horse.

For example, if we want to teach the horse to pick things up or play 'fetch', possible slices to use are: 1. Look at object. 2. Sniff object. 3. Nuzzle object. 4. Put mouth around object. 5. Repeat 4 with the object in different positions. 6. Touch and nuzzle object on the ground. 7. Put mouth around object while it is on the ground. 8. Any suggestion of lifting the head holding the object. 9. Bringing the object up to our hand. 10. Holding the object until we have time to put our hand on it. 11. Releasing the object into our hand. 12. Moving beside us holding the object. 13. Moving toward us holding the object. 14. Moving away from us toward the object on the ground. 15. As 14 plus picking it up. 16. As 15 plus turning and bringing it back to us.

The key is to stay with each slice until the horse is comfortable and confident with it, before moving on to the next slice.

Successive Approximations: We start with what the horse can offer already, and gradually direct and reward each tiny change in the direction of the final behavior* we want. (See 'Slices' and Thin-Slicing.)

Targeting: Asking the horse to put his nose or foot on an object to earn a click&treat.

Thin-slicing: Cutting a task into its smallest teachable (clickable) parts (slices) so we can teach the horse in a way that keeps him being continually successful as much as possible.

Threshold: The point at which we begin to feel uneasy about a situation. Our breathing rate and heart rate increase, we sweat and may get funny feelings in our gut.

The same things happen to horses when they reach threshold. Their confidence turns to anxiety.

The better we are at realizing when horses reach threshold, the more effective our training will be. This is because we can ensure that the horse stays near or at threshold while he is learning, but we don't tip him too far over threshold, turning his responses into fear reactions.

Once a horse or a person is over threshold, constructive learning is no longer possible because anxiety emotions have taken over.

Timing: This is one of the most important aspects of good training. We must time the click (mark) to the exact movement (or stillness) that we seek and follow the click promptly with the food reward. We also time the release of our signal pressure* to correspond with the click.

Sometimes we carefully time a series of pressure-release sequences as part of the overall task, with the click&treat at the end (as in Chapter Eight when we ask for a series of backward steps before we click&treat).

Sometimes we work through a series of chained tasks with a click&treat at the end of the chain. When we teach a chain of related tasks, the horse often learns that each earlier task is the signal or cue for the upcoming task, until the sequence or chain ends with a click&treat and relaxation. For example, cleaning all four feet can become a chain of tasks with a click&treat after all four feet are done.

Tongue Click: A sound made my bouncing the tongue off the roof of the mouth. It is a handy marker sound to use when training horses because it is always with us, makes a fairly consistent sound and leaves the hands free to do other things.

Training Plan: An outline of the possible thin-slices* that we might be able to use to teach a horse a particular task. A Training Plan is the starting point for writing an Individual Education Program (IEP)* that suits a specific handler, the specific horse and the specific training environments that they have available.

Triple Treat: This is something I use as a major celebration when the horse does something really well or has made a breakthrough with a new piece of learning. First, I click&treat for the behavior* performed as usual.

Then I lift a fist into the air and have the horse target my fist for another click&treat. I repeat the 'raised fist target' two more times, making it a 'triple treat'. The triple treat serves both to accentuate a job well done and gives the horse a short break from the concentrated work we've been doing.

Zero Intent: Taking up a body language position that indicates to the horse that we don't want anything to happen; that we are standing or walking together in a relaxed manner (the details are in Chapter Three).

Hertha James

Tiakitahuna, New Zealand

December 2018

hertha.james@xtra.co.nz

www.herthamuddyhorse.com

Printed in Great Britain
by Amazon